PLACES

PLACES

by

Hilaire Belloc

Essay Index Reprint Series

 BOOKS FOR LIBRARIES PRESS
FREEPORT, NEW YORK

824. 91
B446 p

INTERNATIONAL STANDARD BOOK NUMBER:
0-8369-2037-6

LIBRARY OF CONGRESS CATALOG CARD NUMBER:
78-117759

PRINTED IN THE UNITED STATES OF AMERICA

To

DOROTHY COLLINS

Contents

CONTENTS

These essays originally appeared in the following papers:—*The Sunday Times*, *The Tablet*, *The Universe*, *Geographical Magazine*, *Truth*, and *Wine and Food*, to the editors of which journals I owe my thanks for their appearance here between covers.

Introduction

It is a nice question whether ignorance or stupidity plays the greater part in human affairs. In particular, one may well enquire whether the one or the other plays the greater part in the conduct of foreign policy.

It is the great strength and glory of the whole society that we ask no questions and that all goes on without the interference of those who know too much and still better without the interference of those who understand too much. For, after all, what practical good was ever effected by the action of opinion upon foreign policy?

Now and then (once in a blue moon) what is called "public opinion" gets wildly excited about something about which the man in the street knows nothing whatever. Nothing. Nothing. Absolutely nothing. On those rare occasions foreign policy is interfered with by public opinion; but so strong have been the forces in the past of an aristocratic society that the idiots were suppressed. The people who knew absolutely nothing about anything of European affairs were sidetracked (as the Americans have it) or at any rate put into a bag.

Will that happy state of affairs last for ever? In England we take it for granted that it will. But I am not so sure.

Anyhow, we have certainly arrived at the end of a chapter: the chapter of security. Decisions will have to be taken;

not it is to be hoped, by public opinion, but by *somebody.*
The old security is gone.

It does not follow that we ought to attempt an understanding of foreign people today. Probably if we tried to
do that things would get even worse; because they would
become more perilous. And yet one can't help wishing, at
least I can't help wishing, that people in this country knew
more about other people. The great bond would be religion;
but of that bond people today know nothing. A secondary
and much feebler bond is travel.

I am afraid I do not believe very much in the effect of
travel as an aid to wisdom unless it be accompanied by a
profoundly transcendental and universal philosophy. So let
us let the thing slide. A boulder has been set rolling down a
mountain slope. It will bound from rock to rock. It will
pursue its blind course. We shall contemplate the result. It
may be we shall contemplate the ruin. With these profound
and pleasing thoughts I leave you.

I have here collected many an impression of travel of the
sort which I fear can never be repeated in a ruined world.

PLACES

On Frontiers

I HAVE HAD OCCASION TO CROSS A NUMBER OF FRONTIERS IN the course of travel, from Portugal into Spain, from Spain into France, from France into Italy and into Belgium, and so on. And every time this experience befalls me (which is commonly many times a year) certain things arise in my mind.

The first is this: that frontiers are things recent. We think of them now as at once sacred and, in the case of the older nations, permanent. Yet there was a time (not so long ago) when they were not. Now that we have substituted the worship of the nation for older forms of worship there is, naturally, a sanctity about national frontiers, but it was not always so.

It is difficult to imagine oneself back in those days— less than three centuries ago—when frontiers such as we now know them meant nothing to the ordinary man. There was not between one realm and another any very definite boundary. The nations had arisen out of a feudal system which was a chaos of local lordships. One group of these would get attached to one supreme overlord and king. But men did not think of themselves primarily as the citizens of this or that nation. They thought of themselves as the subjects, or more often the feudal dependents, of this or that authority. The feeling of fellowship went by language, by religion, by local customs, by all manner of things

3

other than the imaginary lines which have now become so important upon the map, and may, a few generations hence, have lost that importance again.

One often hears of "natural frontiers." Much blood has been shed and whole libraries written in defence of that conception. But the truth is that natural frontiers are very rare. A river, even a great river, is commonly inhabited by much the same kind of people on either bank, and a range of mountains hardly ever divides people neatly one from the other. The Pyrenees, one would have thought, of all the ranges in Europe, would best serve this purpose. Yet in the Catalan country the political frontier between France and Spain is wholly artificial, drawn up less than three hundred years ago. The watershed is vague; you cross it without noticing it, on a sort of tumbled flattish land. The same language is talked and the same domestic habits are found in all that country, whether in the part that is marked Spanish on the map or the part marked French. Navarre lies astraddle of the range; so does the Basque tongue and race. The Garonne rises in Spanish soil. Its upper waters run through the Val d'Aran and are not politically French but Spanish; yet as you walk down the course of the stream you see little difference in the people.

The Alps do not form a true dividing line either. Much of the valley of Aosta talked French and felt French till the modern Italian kingdom arose. And everybody knows the way in which a territory of German speech and habits overflows the boundary of the Brenner, making the Southern Tyrol (which is geographically Italian) a thing German in social character.

I myself knew as a boy old men to whom the division between what is now Belgium and what is now Holland seemed quite artificial, the result of the successful revolt of the Southern Netherlands against the Dutch Royal Family, imposed upon them after the defeat of Napoleon. The ultimate cause of the division between the two parts of the Low Countries was religious, yet the boundary is not a boundary of religion at all. It was set up, more or less arbitrarily, in the seventeenth century to safeguard the commercial interests of Holland from French overlordship, and to ratify the success of the earlier Dutch rebellion against Spanish rule.

What is now North-Eastern France, the Department of the Nord (what used to be called French Flanders), was, almost within living memory, indistinguishable from the people of similar speech on the other side of the frontier between France and Belgium. That political frontier stood, with a few brief exceptions, as it was laid down after the conquests of Louis XIV. Yet it was only in the nineteenth century, especially after the coming of elementary universal education, that French Flanders became socially distinct from the Flemish district just beyond. Lille was once as Flemish as Ypres; and I can remember myself as a child hearing Flemish spoken as far West as the fish market of Calais. It is still spoken, of course, in Dunkerque.

What is more surprising is to find that local loyalties were quite different not so many generations ago from what they have since become. Alsace is a classic example, but there are more surprising earlier ones: for instance, the country round Bordeaux and to the south of it. The wine districts of the Gironde, and Bordeaux itself, long regretted their lost connection with the English Crown, and Henry VIII in his youth toyed with the idea of reoccupying all that part of the old Plantagenet realm. The trade of Bordeaux was with England, the town was lightly taxed, all its profit lay in the English connection. When the French kings entered at the end of the Middle Ages, they entered as conquerors, and not very welcome conquerors at that. It would have astonished our fathers to have heard the violence of modern discussion upon frontiers, and I am fairly certain that it will astonish posterity as much as it seems natural to us.

It has been part of the making of England that the realm had only one land frontier, and that short and of an uncertain kind. All bounds elsewhere were of the sea. This frontier, if it can be called a frontier, was the Border—vague like all such marches, until quite modern times. But the people north of the Border were foreigners to the people south of it all the same. That apparently was why Charles II failed in his march before the battle of Worcester in the effort to restore his throne. None rose to help an invader.

Frontiers will cease to be sacred some time hence. How long a time I know not: but I should give them no very great lease. Already differences of class interest are beginning to count as much or more than nationalism in one Continental industrial district after another. When the next great religious change comes (it is long overdue) that also will play its part in differentiating one human group from another. Most of the invisible lines drawn artificially today across a real countryside have no true permanence in them.

Fashion

I WONDER WHAT THE NEXT FASHION IN TRAVEL WILL BE?
Literary travel I mean, the travel that produces books.

For a very long time literary fashion used travel only
in its original function: that of getting from one place to
another. The most interesting journeys of the Middle Ages,
and much the most of those in antiquity, tell you of towns
and places, but not of hills and their aspect nor of distant
horizons on the way.

That was certainly the longest-lived fashion, and it was
not till modern times that this fashion changed, and that
men began to record the road as well as the place to which
the road led, and the country to the sides of the road, and
the changing aspects of the world through which they
passed. This fashion began, one may fairly say, at the end
of the ·sixteenth century, and there are fragments of it
found throughout the seventeenth, especially towards the
end of that age; but for a spate of it (a spate which
has not yet run off) Western Europe had to wait for
what is called the "Romantic Revival," though why
"Romantic" I do not know. It was a new mood altogether.

When that mood fell upon an enthusiastic generation
(that which preceded and introduced the French Revolution), writers began to wallow in the picturesque, the

sublime, the strange, the remote, and all manner—so only that it were not human.

Before the Romantic Revival, before your Wordsworth and my—(never mind who; why should I divulge my private reading?) there was plenty of travel interest in characters, and before that, in people and places combined. The whole of the Picaresque is based upon that theme— men, especially the oddity of men, and the writer's experience of men as he moves about. The main interest of the traveller was still a human interest. With the last half of the eighteenth century his interest became an interest human only in so far as it recorded the effect of inanimate nature upon his own isolated soul.

From that day to this, the literature of wandering has been crammed with the pathetic fallacy, ascribing to inanimate nature the quality of joy and suffering which is proper to living animals, and especially to animals with souls—among whom we reckon mankind—but not to rocks and streams. I have read many explanations of why there came this sudden transition in the emotional literature of Christendom, but no explanation has ever satisfied me. It is a fact that a man will write home at any time in the seventeenth century or in the earlier eighteenth, and in his letters talk of marbles, of painting, or arches and columns, of ruins, or great officers in Church and State whom he is privileged to meet (or, more often, to see from far off). He will tell you exactly enough the appearance and manner of a Pope or great noble, a famous writer or general, or even a wretched stuffed prince, but you hear little of what happens between one centre of human beings and another, save occasionally complaint of the extravagant charges and bad entertainment of an inn.

That same man's son will write from abroad in a totally

different fashion. He is all rocks and waterfalls and big hills and stretches of champaign and the majesty of mighty rivers. With these he will infuse, even in private letters, a certain personal melancholy, not to say peevishness, and when he is writing, not for a private eye, but for the public, he returns to his own tragedies. That was the great mark of the romantic time, I think; a naive, often exasperating preoccupation with the writer's little troubles. They seemed great ones to him, but why should we trouble about them? Later on, this inordinate complaint with the general lot turned sour and became worse, it bred a taste for horrors and all manner of misfortunes, mainly sordid. But still the fashion for the inanimate world, presumed to be animate by a fiction, survived. It is going full blast today in the angry complaint against the sordid surroundings which, none the less, our moderns love to dwell upon as well as to dwell amid.

So far so good, or, rather, so bad. Let me return to my original theme which started all this. What is going to succeed the romantic phase, now in its putrescence? After the degradation of what the French call naturalism (which simply means talking about things which ought not to be talked about, and is, in effect, the most unnatural thing in the world: witness Zola), what is going to be the new stunt?

Pray note the following most interesting truth: *People cannot imagine the future because they cannot but believe that experience has been exhausted.* All fiction portraying the future fills it with contemporaries, sometimes changed in dress, but still contemporaries. For instance, very few such books portray a new religion, and when they do so, that religion has no flame in it. Yet when a novel phase comes, it proves to be as vital as it is new.

Well, what will it be? I know what I should like it to

be (but what I am pretty certain it will not be). I should like our next literary fashion to be real and visualised history, particularly military history. I should like the writer on distant places and lesser known tracks at home to tumble by the same way of interest into the road of battles and campaigns. Heaven knows there is material enough! I cannot promise you that I shall not myself some day break out into a picture of, say, Naseby or Dunbar.

However, I say the vogue for real and living military history is an unlikely development. Will it be religion, which I have just called neglected? The history of religion, the passions roused by religious controversy? Not yet: all is still bad form. And note you that daring pioneers of literature are terrified of bad form. Will it be mere merchandise: travel for gain? That *motif* has appeared in much fiction, it might appear in the relation of actual experience. Will it be *discovery*? "No," you answer, "for there is nothing more to be discovered." To which I answer: "Yes there is, burrowing underground as in 'The Coming Race,' or plunging into the depths of the sea like the 'Nautilus.'" Some new fashion will come. It is long overdue. What will it be? The best answer to that question, as to all things concerning the future, is, "We do not know, we cannot know, and the less we pretend to know the less the chance of making fools of ourselves."

On Wandering

I HAVE WANDERED ALL MY LIFE, AND I HAVE ALSO TRAVELLED; the difference between the two being this, that we wander for distraction, but we travel for fulfilment.

A man wanders in order to entertain himself with new discoveries and experiences, the stranger the better, and if beautiful, why then better still. But he travels in order to visit cities and men, and to get a knowledge of the real places where things happened in the past, getting a knowledge also of how the mind of man worked in building and works now in daily life. The two things overlap, do wandering and travel. In all travel there is some element of wandering, though often very little travel in wandering is undertaken for its own sake. Yet are the two distinct.

A man travels most fully if he has already learned much of the place he would visit. The goal of his journey when it reaches it, is thus already furnished for him; yet however thoroughly he knows a place in this secondary way it will be still quite new to him when he discovers it in reality. There is nothing more striking about travel than this: that not only scenes and buildings with which a man is—or thinks himself to be—familiar from much reading, but even those which have been reproduced a thousand times until they are quite hackneyed, turn out, upon discovery of them, to be new and unsuspected things.

There is a landscape which is perhaps the most repeated

in the world, and which modern men have seen in photography reproduced in series. It is the sight of Vesuvius seen from the shoulder of the hill of Naples. Yet when I saw it for the first time in my thirtieth year I found it to be a thing quite different from what I was awaiting. The volcano seemed to overhang all the city and the plain about it; it was the person of that country, and Naples was but an attendant thereto. There was a slight wisp of smoke from the crater, such as I had read of I know not how often, but to *see* it was to see a wholly novel thing. It was as though in all that lay before one the mountain alone was sombrely alive. This novelty about a distant place actually experienced at last through the senses is not due to the addition of sight and sound and scent, temperature, and the movement of the actual air. It is not the filling in of an outline or the embodiment of a vision hitherto vague, it is what I have called it, a discovery. So much is it a discovery that for each newcomer it is a discovery of his own.

I have known men who have gone so far in their fear of disappointment and their disgust with mere repetition that they deliberately avoided visiting whatever had filled modern fiction and illustration, especially whatever had been hammered in by advertisements. One such went out of his way to miss the Pyramids. They who act thus are comprehensible enough, yet they are wrong. If the man who had avoided the Pyramids had seen those great kilns, he would probably have come back with something quite new which would remain fresh with him to the end of his life. He might, for instance, have found them disappointingly small, though I am told that the largest of them would cover Lincoln's Inn Fields.

As for the Acropolis of Athens, I knew yet another man

who, determining to avoid it, thought he had seen it rising in splendid fashion through the half light from the harbour of the Piraeus a little before true dawn had come, and while things were still grey. He was profoundly moved; he repented of his foolish and deliberate isolation, and became inspired with something like worship. As the light broadened, the outline puzzled him, and long before it was full day he discovered the sacred rock to be, in fact, a neighbouring warehouse, with a penthouse for the Parthenon and a few chimney-pots for columns. Yet when he came to see the true Acropolis later on that same day he was very pleased. For he had the good fortune to come upon it from the North, in which aspect it is a rock indeed. But famous things seen in travel are most effective, I think, when they are unexpected. Let me repeat here such an experience of travel long ago.

I was in a train, travelling through the raw and chilly air of the very early morning before the spring had come upon Tuscany. I was intent upon reaching, for dull political reasons, a further place where it was my duty to discuss dull political things in a dull exposition which I knew well would bear no fruit. Happily for me, the train stopped in the middle of a wide expanse through some small accident or other. I was told that we had at least an hour to wait, and there began the noise of distant hammering. With other passengers I got out of the train, to taste the freshness of the air, and I saw, almost on a level with my eye, the level line of water under hills which marks a lake. I asked of a fellow-traveller, native to that country, what the name of that mere might be—it was only curiosity; I hardly wanted to know—when he replied with a word which struck me like a clap of thunder: "Trasimene." I was to see that famous lake many, many a time in later years; I was even to go carefully over the supposed site of the battle between the shore and the lifted land beyond, but no further acquaintance, no increase of detail, came near to that first revelation.

The moral would seem to be, travel with an object, travel with exact intention, and be certain that you will be rewarded on the way by some discovery inward and outward much beyond your expectation.

That is one of the fifteen or sixteen hundred ways in which passage through the places of the earth is like passage through a human life and in which travel so closely follows the pattern of living. For in life we both know and do not know what it is that we approach, and find accidental revelation perpetually, as well as accidental disappointment.

I take it that the wise are those who do not too much allow natural frailty to emphasise the disappointments, but who are careful to record for their own enrichment the happier accidents along with the less happy. Though there is, it is true, this trouble about the better things, that they do not last. So it is with the worse, as well as the better. But we forget that consolation.

Perhaps the best relaxation for the mind is the recollection of normal and familiar travel not too far from home. It is one of the worst of the minor evils attaching to great modern wars that they cut men off from recreative travel. Cultivated British people of a past and happier generation never showed their taste and wisdom more than in their fashion of travel. The Victorian period was full of wise use in this respect, and the conversation of my elders was filled with experience of the Continent, more civilised than their own land. From the beginning of the railway era, and even before, there was no better or stronger cultural influence than this occupation of leisure by travel.

Even before the catastrophe of 1914 and the opening of the first Great War of our time, travel had become less valuable.

It was deteriorating. Much larger numbers travelled and they travelled less intelligently because they forgot more and more the object of travel, which is a mixture of information, novelty and enlargement. These are most fully obtained when men and women already sufficiently instructed in the past go from one European town to another, staying in those inns and hotels which are full of local custom and tradition.

Today we mark with regret the contrast between those older days of our early youth and the first years of the twentieth century. The big cosmopolitan hotels of that later time were no centres for real travel. The French have a generic term for such hotels, the term "palace," and I think it would be well to have a generic term for them all over Europe. They gave the same cooking pretty well everywhere, and it was mediocre. They had much the same furniture. They had the same atmosphere of regular and mechanical living, which was death to all hospitality and to all domestic feeling. Therefore the wise continued to patronise such of the older hostelries as were left; but these also dwindled one by one and the first sign of death in them was the appearance of the American bar.

I am not sure that travelling by stage-coach, of which we have made a romance nowadays, was better worthwhile than the slower kind of Victorian travel by train. I talked a good deal with my elders when I was young about their stage-coach experiences and they were never enthusiastic about them. They nearly all agreed that the railway had come as a relief. Even those who were wealthy enough to use the post-chaise—such as that in which my English grandfather travelled over a great part of France and Italy with my mother in her youth—did not feel the coming of the railway to be a loss of opportunity save in one point: that of landscape.

I have heard men and women of that generation say that no one has really appreciated Italy since the Alps were pierced. Crossing the mountains by the high summer roads one saw the new vision of the southern land open before one and there was the right interval between the North and South. But except in this point of international travel, all but a few of that generation agreed that the railway, which they came to use more and more during and after the 'fifties, had given them a greater possession of Europe than had the older forms of travel.

I cannot help feeling also that the guide-books of the Victorian time made better reading and told one much more than those of our day. I preserve and, so long as travel was possible, used in travel the old Murrays and Baedekers which I had inherited. They were well written; they told one the things one really wanted to know. So did the travel books of those days, which were a time of discovery after a fashion: notably a discovery of what mountains could mean. One of the best books ever written in that connection was Whymper's *Scrambles Among the Alps*. There was a sense of height and majesty in his illustrations which we do not get today. But I am afraid the best of all that travel period—the end of which I well remember, for by the end of the century and of the reign I had already experienced my best travel years from the time when I was only seventeen—can never be restored.

One can often still go off by a side-track to some little-known district and recover in part the atmosphere of those days. One can have in many countrysides the full tradition of a quiet and happy civilisation with a prosperous agriculture for its background and a long tradition of architecture showing upon every side. But one cannot get away from the wireless or from the gramophone. You will suffer even in the remotest hamlets that assault on the nerves which is a permanent character of modern competitive publicity.

I remember once in a barber's shop of the most primitive kind up in the high Pyrenees, where there was no road but only a rough stone mule-track leading to the little group of houses, having before me while I was being shaved a violently-coloured picture imploring me in American to buy a particular brand of bicycle. What tenacious travelling salesman could have planted such a thing in such a place? There it was and I have always remembered it— which after all was what the advertiser wanted me to do, I suppose.

On Travel During War

I HAVE HAD OCCASION TO TRAVEL CONSIDERABLY, THOUGH only over a restricted field, during three periods of war, and only three: the period of the Great War of a quarter of a century ago, a few months of the present war, and a part of the civil war in Spain. In the first of these periods I saw nothing outside France and Italy until the Armistice, after which I saw a good deal of the Reich and something of Austria, and something of Poland, after which I had a brief experience of travel during the war in Spain.

Experience of this kind is so much less than that which the regular war correspondent enjoys that I am diffident in using it for a text; yet there are certain things I have noticed in the course of these war-time travels which I retain as useful to an understanding of the modern world, and as emphasising the contrast between war and peace.

The main thing, of course, which impresses the mind during travel in war-time over the territory of a country involved in hostilities is the contrast in human uses. You have the same instruments, the same landscapes, but the human society occupied with those instruments and the landscape upon which it lives and moves are under a spell. It is as though a magical effect had transformed the common purposes of men. Those common purposes continue, save in the very field of battle itself, or in areas immediately subjected to destructive attack. There are the same monuments, the same fields, the same methods of progress, the same public sheets for information. But all under a kind of silence and inhibition.

It is not so much a climate of fear that has affected the common air as a climate of arrest. It is as though everyone were waiting for something other than the things immediately presented to the senses. That is the general note: a halt and an expectation, each, both the interruption and the awaiting, of an utterly different kind from what one had known for a life-time in those same hills, on those same plains, in those same villages and towns. The sensation never leaves one; even when every evidence of warfare is absent there is always that feeling, "in a moment all this may change."

Another powerful effect of war upon travel is the contrast between the application of similar physical sensations.

I recall one example of this very vividly. The silence of the English Downs where they are most empty, just above the entry into the Narrows of the Channel. Those wide and singularly untenanted spaces—untenanted of men at least—still hear the plover calling on the marshes, the wind in the beech trees, and the bleating of the sheep; but much more dim, so dim as to be hardly recognised, there may be other sounds, which had never been heard there before. Thus here on those same heights there came to me during the main English offensive in Flanders, the very distant roll of something that might have been thunder, so far off as to be hardly heard. It was the guns, up-weather, for the day was one on which the wind was from the southeast.

A totally different experience of travel in war is the sense of continual interruption, not unlike that which a man feels when, in familiar surroundings, he finds himself disturbed by unexpected action and new, unexplained causes of attention. Looking back, it is astonishing how few are those occasions, and yet how striking they can be.

But among all my thoughts as I have travelled in civilian fashion during war-time has been this major question: "What will be the fruit to history of all this? How will such a hiatus affect that human story by which all hitherto have lived?"

Will not myths arise much more monstrous, much more irrational, than those older myths which we ridiculed in the days of our security and intellectual pride?

Remember that in war-time information is cut off at the source. All that general secondary experience which was taken as a matter of course in European life until the great shock of 1914, all that we got by the Press and by a steady stream of descriptive books, and by compared relations of things seen and heard, ceased abruptly.

What is more, it ceases in sections. One large body of human beings has one whole field of information cut off; another, another. How can one make any unity or establish any general judgment in such grotesque partial flashes? Will not perhaps our whole national picture of the time through which we have lived be at once so broken and so destroyed as to be no picture at all? In that case, our immediate posterity will have no one general conclusion on which to base life, only a welter of contradictory follies. It was bad enough to see what false history was written through the exaggeration of national feeling, through the conflict of religious emotions, and through the fragmentary imperfection of even modern record. But what will it be when we are faced with nothing but a mass of contradictions, and when, looking for evidence, we come to nothing but calculated falsehood?

This is what seems to me the grave, perhaps the gravest, evil of our time. For history is always somewhat false, and by its falsehood always somewhat warps judgment; but history written on the basis of deliberate falsehood and of repeated and prolonged suppression would be another matter altogether. It would not be history at all.

Now history is the memory of the race; and a man without memory is no longer a man.

On History in Travel

THERE ARE THREE WAYS OF TREATING TRAVEL IN CONNECTION
with history. The first way (which naturally commends
itself to the present stage of our civilisation) is to travel
with no knowledge of history whatsoever. You go to
Worcester, for instance, and you see a big church which
is called a cathedral, but you do not know what that word
means in history. There was a battle fought there which
ended the Civil Wars, but you have never heard of it, so
you do not worry. You pass through Rome, staying a
night or two, and you see some curious old ruins, some of
them very large, a good deal of quaint architecture, plenty
of gilding, another enormous church, and quite a number
of very large private houses. You also see certain arches
and a conspicuous column, and so on. Wherever you go
you see things as a child sees them. A picturesque thing
or a striking site will remain in your memory, but you will
not trouble about its significance, its growth, its setting in
the present or its possible effect upon the future. That is
one very good way of treating history in travel. When I
was young I did a lot of it myself, and it furnished my mind
with a number of excellent, vivid pictures which I still
retain.

The second way of treating travel in combination with
history is to go to a place of which you have read a very

great deal. Suppose you go, for instance, to Vicenza, and you are interested in architecture as well as in history; you see nothing very striking to the eye—at least, nothing specially outstanding; but your reading enables you to go into all the details of the Palladian architecture. You see it there at its summit. You notice a thousand things that the common traveller hardly sees, and you go away with your reading enlivened and made real by visual experience. You make your headquarters at a very good hotel in the middle of the town and stay there a week or a fortnight, drawing and poking about. You come back vastly enriched. Incidentally you may remark the influence of that long, peaceable Venetian rule which so singularly resembled the rule of commercial England over her countrysides. Perhaps you push on to Este and its high, conical hills, from the defence of which arose that very ancient family, the Estes, who married into the Guelphs and occupied for generations the Throne of England, and you so come back further enriched.

The third way of treating travel and history combined is, I think, the best: it is to take travel in connection with general history and to recognise wherever you go the stages of that majestic process. Thus a man needs no very deep learning but a certain breadth of it, to enjoy Sicily in this fashion. If he knows something, a mere outline, of the Greek colonial history; of the Carthaginian wars, especially the first Carthaginian war, of the coming of Islam on to the Mediterranean, of the Norman establishment, and of the brief French moment, later in the Middle Ages, of the subsequent Spanish establishment, of the rise of the new Italy and the Garibaldian business—all that he sees informs him through the eye and establishes in a concrete form what had been before mere reading. Palermo lives for him; so does Syracuse; the great isolated height of Castrogiovanni with its memories of the Servile War and its vast central view over the island to distant Etna; Trapani, and Butler's fantastic theory of the Odyssey; Girgenti, and the rest—all these come alive. So do Catania and Taormina, and he can appreciate in a new manner what is meant by the Straits of Messina. He may even be amused by the little eddy which was once Charybdis. Such a journey with such general information for the foundation of it is fruitful indeed. He need be no scholar, he need have no great possession of detail, but he will come back full of stuff, and he will never forget Cefalu, where he may busy himself with guess-work upon the origin of that marvellous, packed theological epigram, an hexameter and a pentameter which, if I remember right after so many years, runs round the half dome of the mosaic in the Apse.

This last way of combining history with travel is, I think, the best. It is open to any man of reasonable culture, free from pedantry and awake to the things of the eye. This kind of travel, like all travel, to be fruitful needs maps; they need not be large-scale maps, a very general scheme of the island's geography with its names is sufficient.

The first of these methods of travel is not to be despised; it is at the call of everyone, and I think on the whole it gives the sharpest memories; it also provides one with discoveries; one sees things for the first time, which, though one does not know what they are, leave a powerful impression upon the mind and later, on one's return, one can fill up such impressions with further reading. The second method is for scholars only and for specialists who know their subject thoroughly before starting. Actual experience of an external thing always proves it to be something different from what had been imagined in the course of one's reading, and travel of that kind fills up all the interstices of such reading, as it were, and gives complete knowledge of one's particular subject. But the third method, I repeat, is still the best: go forth with general knowledge in your mind, not worrying yourself too much over particulars, regarding disputed questions as matters for debate rather than for settlement, and saying to yourself as you move about. "So this is where such and such a thing happened! This is where such and such a famous man stood, or warred, or died."

If, by way of conclusion, you want to know the worst way of treating travel so far as its historical content and value is concerned, I should say that the worst way to travel was with nothing but official or conventional history in your mind. For instance, if you travel through Spain in a mood furnished by the conventional textbook version of Spanish history, thinking of Spain as a country once Gothic, then Mohammedan, then Christian again, knowing nothing of its permanent traditions and people underneath, you will not be able to make head or tail of it. But I have come to the end of this essay, and there is no space to say, even most briefly, what the Romanisation of the Peninsula, the conversion of the Empire, the Gothic mercenaries and their leaders, the Islamic governments and the Reconquista really were.

An Episode of War

THOSE WHO ARE FAMILIAR WITH THE LESS FAMOUS DIARIES and memoirs of rather more than a hundred years ago (the diaries and memoirs of the First Empire in France and of pre-Waterloo England) will bear witness to the interesting fact that in the midst of such tremendous events the writers noticed, sometimes with a passionate interest, nearly always with curious interest, comparatively slight incidents which had nothing to do with the awful main current of their time. It is a commonplace that in much of the fiction, and notably in the novels of Jane Austen, you will find this detachment from what we in retrospect consider to be the only things of that day worth remembering.

There was a moment in the Great War (some time in 1917, I think) when I happened to be visiting an observation post up among the tall fir-trees of the Vosges. It was a wooden platform perched above the world among the higher branches and led up to dizzily by a succession of ladders, which I had painfully mounted under the orders and guidance of a French colonel who had been asked to look after me. When I got to the platform I was introduced to a major and another officer, whose rank I forget, who were occupied in observation and were using a large telescope turned on to the German lines below.

The platform was not visible to the enemy, of course. It was screened by heavy boughs; but the end of the tele-

scope was clear of obstacles and they invited me to look
through it. I did so. It was a bright summer's day in a moment when everything was quiet on this sector, and I had
before me a very vivid, highly coloured, little circular picture, magnified by I do not know how many diameters.
I was watching a scene several miles away. And what I saw
was a worthy German of middle age dressed up in his field-
grey, unarmed, and toiling painfully up a sandy path in
the hills with two heavy pails full of water, grasped by
the handle in each hand. The double burden balanced him,
but it nearly overbalanced him as well. He stuck to his task
manfully enough; then he put down the pails for a minute,
mopped his forehead and puffed. But he puffed in dumb
show, for not a sound could cross the intervening gulf of
distance. He was Beyond the Veil. I watched him take his
two pails up again and go round a bend in the path—and
I never saw him again.

I am no good at verbal suggestion and I despair of con-
veying to my reader how deeply this insignificant moment
etched itself into my memory. I can see it now as intensely
as I saw it then—the sunlight, the dark trees, the mountain
path, the distant plain and the reservist in his field-grey.
We were nothing to each other—but I hope he survived.

When I took my eye away from the telescope I had not
occupied it for more than a couple of minutes, for I was
both an intruder and a guest. My host, the major, clapped
an eye in his turn on to the eyepiece and told me the number of the enemy division which lay in that sector.

Then the colonel, who was, as I have said, my guide, and
also gave me orders, asked me whether I would like to see
a tame bird which the men of a neighbouring post farther
down the mountain, and on the sheltered side thereof, had
trained to perform—that is, to sing—for their entertainment. We walked some way downhill westward through

the forest until we came to a high road where the motor was waiting for us. We went forward for a mile or two through the wood and the colonel got out at an open glade. He led me on about a couple of hundred yards to a place where I found a number of men gathered listening to the little beast on the bough. I know nothing about birds. I cannot tell you the name of this one. I did not find its song particularly pleasing; but what I did find pleasing was the innocent, childlike pleasure which all those warriors took in the performance; and one of them on the edge of the group turned to me and asked with enthusiasm whether I did not think it wonderful for a man to have got a bird to be so familiar with his captors and so willing to sing for them.

I did. But I thought it much more wonderful that men who but a few days before had been in the battle-line were thus taking their pleasure in the deep, silent woods, wherein from time to time sounded from far away a casual gun.

I remember also how the silence was accompanied by the busy prattle of a mountain stream that came along tumbling and cascading through the sandy bed of the forest and making itself out to be the most important thing in the world.

That evening I ate with a number of officers and heard the fragments of the news from that part of the line, notably of a diary which had been found on the body of some poor young German gentleman who had been killed in action a week or two before. The sentences were commonplace enough, but they profoundly moved me, coming as they did from the dead. There was no word about his home or about the cause for which he died; only one rather amusing passage stood out in which he expressed astonishment at the short stature of the French, which seemed to have made them, in his eyes, unfit for war. For the rest, those pencilled pages were but brief daily records. There was no disloyalty in examining them; for they were public matter for the Intelligence.

That night I slept in one of those neat cottages on the heights between Alsace and Lorraine; a place used for the occasional visitor, such as I was. My guide passed the night under the same roof. A soldier made our coffee for us in the morning and we went off through the fresh, cold, mountain air of sunrise, down, down, down into the plains.

Many things did I see, in the course of those four years and more, between the Adriatic and the Channel, along that immense line broken only by the Swiss frontier; but none of the things I saw has remained with me as strongly marked as the chance experience of that day.

South and North

It is pleasant in mid-winter, here in the North, to call to mind the gardens of the South and their amenity, even though there be some illusion about this. For the truth is that the climate of southern England is the best in Europe. I do not say the best granted to man, for I have heard that there are places in the Pacific isles which are like Paradise, and I myself have known mountain slopes in California that were an introduction to Eden. But I did not know those hills of California all the year round, and I do know both how intolerably hot the Mohave can be and how treacherous the cold mist rolling into the bay from the Pacific. When we say that the climate of south England is the best in the world we mean that it fits in best with man's nature, day in and day out throughout all the seasons of the year. Only it has received a bad name and, therefore, is, I suppose, ripe for hanging.

But, as we certainly lack sun and suffer in the winter months as a rule from dampness, it is no wonder that we look back on our memories of the sun, when the North is too much for us. And, indeed, if we could fix the best days of the South, escaping the great heats or the sudden cold which often strikes it unnaturally, we should find living in the Mediterranean air a better place than this. Yet, for my part, having had plenty of that air in all seasons, I still find myself best in south England, especially when all earth and sky are invigorated by the south-west wind roaring in from the Atlantic, which is, I think, the presiding genius of England.

The gardens of the South have everything to be said for them when all is in tune. Yet have I known in those latitudes and on that earth very intolerable cold as well as heat. I remember well one day when I walked, not of my own choice, over the hills from the Lake of Bolsena to Orvieto against so bitter a blast of sleet and driving snow that it needed all one's courage to push on. It was like being in Scotland without the fun.

(For I am one of those who always think it fun to be in Scotland.)

And I remember another occasion when a friend and I nearly froze to death motoring on the edges of the Sahara Desert. Nor was it early in the year. It was already March, and, if I remember right, rather late in March. We were crossing at high speed one of those plains where the Mohammedan has destroyed all trees, a district which before the coming of Islam had been wooded and fertile, nourishing great cities and pleasant villas of the Roman rich; but now half waste and only distinguished here and there by vast ruins. The wind was so abominably keen that it almost made one wish to stop living. What was extraordinary, it was not a wind from any northern point; it blew straight out of the desert. I take it that it was air which had fallen in a sort of cascade from the upper heaven where it is always cold, had been sucked in suddenly into the lower strata or perhaps sent to be a trial to us under the orders of Azrael, the Angel of Death.

And yet another time, visiting some mines not very high up in the foothills of Atlas, I found the cold so fearful at that same season of the year that there was no dealing with it. Yet it is true that to come on to the Mediterranean land in what is their early spring and what is our late winter is a most heartening thing. Time and again have I had the sense of resurrection when, having left not an hour before the desperate North on the wrong side of the Alps, I came in through a hole in the ground to the upper valley of some Lombard stream. But of all such contrasts recommend me not so much the descent upon Italy as the run down from Reno into the majesty and wealth of the Sierras. Stevenson wrote a famous passage on it, and he was right.

Now the reverse of the medal is this: that the Mediterranean lands, especially those of the Levant, may be perfectly damnable for heat that is not human at all but more like an oven than like any breathable air; and this abomination may come upon one quite early in the season. I seem to remember that it was on a first of May I was struck by a blast of this kind in the outskirts of Jerusalem and found it not tolerable at all. It made one want to get away from the world altogether. One felt oneself in the grasp of some power actively evil. The trial was such that I remember getting to the sunlit side of a wall rather than remain on the shadowed side where the air was more still and, therefore, more abominably torrid.

I was told that they call this kind of air the "Hamsun." Whatever its name, if you have once felt it you can never forget it. It makes you wonder that men live at all in lands where such things can happen. It reminded me of the worthy merchant who had not before travelled and who struck an earthquake by night after his first day in Monte Carlo; after which he said that what with losing his money and his sense of earthly security for ever—I mean his bodily security, his feeling that the world was solid—he might as well have stayed at home in Streatham.

Then there is the Sirocco, a horror which the man born

to more pleasant southern lands, such as the lovely littoral of Sicily, takes for granted, but which is a sort of morticule or little death to you and me. It is not so much the heat, though that is bad enough; it is the air full of dust and the soul full of foreboding and the general misery of nature under that affliction. Then there is the wind called, according to various regions, the Tramontana; and at its fiercest in the funnel of the Rhone Valley, the Mistral. Not only do the people of Provence take the Mistral for granted; they actually make a sort of god of it, and the greatest of their poets took it for a romantic name of his own and his work is known under it so completely that no one remembers what his real name was.

Yet to those who are not of Provence the Mistral is a deadly sword. It sweeps over the earth, not like a wind but like a charge of demons, with a violence and hellish cold combined that are not of this world, and, mind you, it does not come at this or that season; it will fall upon you in any moment, coming over and over again under a steel blue sky, careless of whether it be winter or summer so long as it may work its evil on mankind. I was told by a native of those parts that they expected it on about a third of the days of the year. Perhaps he lied from a genial desire to boast of his native devils, as who should say, "Ha! You have no devils like ours in your milk-and-water country!" But certainly it does blow a great number of days in the year, and it is as pitiless as a hungry she-wolf.

Having gone over most of Europe in all weathers and much of Canada and the United States, I can confidently make this recommendation. If you have the good fortune to live in the south of England do not leave it for very long: but avoid the towns.

The Silences

IF YOU WOULD COMMUNE WITH THE DEAD AND PEOPLE solitude with shades, you will find your best opportunity in deep woods, and these, for preference, upon the less arid slope of a mountain range or of high hills. There, and there alone, you may wholly cut yourself away from the disturbance of human society and the perpetual recurrent catch and pull and drag of daily things. A man can only talk of his own experience, and those who have known the desert best tell me that they find such isolation complete in the desert. I have never found it so; perhaps because I did not go far enough into the waste of sand, perhaps because I did not stay there long enough, but more, I think, from another cause, which was the way in which the desert looms over a man and obsesses him. He is not alone; he is imprisoned, or at least captured by something vast and not wholly impersonal; maleficent.

Of the sea it is certainly true that no man will find solitude there. On the contrary, it was made for adventure of every kind and breeds adventure as swarmingly as it breeds every kind of life. The most absolute calm at sea, however prolonged, gives something very different from the sense of repose. This is perhaps because the sea was never the habitation of men and never can be so.

But the great woods give one all that gift of isolation, in so far as it can be enjoyed at all upon this earth, and they have in them an inhabiting silence. One might add "an inhabited silence," for spirits return there and they are companionable. The trees are brotherly to man, especially the greater trees.

But one must pick and choose to find one's forest places in the Old World, the busy world of Europe to which we belong. Here there will be too many already acquainted with the range, and there an insufficiency of woodland. There are parts of the Atlas where you will find the thing, and even of the Apennines. But the greater part of the African mountains are dry and bare, the central Italian hills are for the most part fully peopled. The Alps, at least the Western Alps, have been captured by human society, and not of the best kind. For my part, the silent places to which I would still return with a fair confidence that I should find myself in that companionship which consoles one for living are best sought on the eastern slope of the Vosges and on the northern slopes of the Pyrenees. The southern slopes of these (when they shall be reopened for travel) are so struck by the sun in the long summer and so unkindly to woodland that they seem (as has often been said of all these heights) an introduction to Africa. But the northern slopes nourish forest upon forest, a belt too wide to be degraded and, in spite of modern things, not so accessible as to be disturbed.

Of course, if you can go far afield you will find isolation at its best in that vast world of heights which overlooks the Pacific for I know not how many hundreds or thousands of miles, Canadian, Californian, and of Oregon and Washington. There also that element which is of the first value in such a quest, the magnitude of the trees, is more triumphantly present than in any other region I know. I have heard even more superb, more regal, more extended, are those of the Himalayas, but these I have never seen.

Meanwhile, for us here in Europe it is the Vosges, especially on their Rhine-ward side, that summon the man who would enjoy that full companionship not to be discovered save in the silent places. Those valleys which descend from the main range, guarded by their ranks upon ranks of enormous conifers, holding small streams and disclosing in one turn after another the plain below and the Black Forest far away (the opposing wall), guard villages and little towns where the life of man seems to be at its best. Nor is human habitation so frequent that the sense of the woodland is interrupted. A man may walk here for days and camp or, in the better weather, sleep out night after night. He returns even after a few days of it as from a better and more secure world. In the rare places where the mountain waters have spread sufficiently to make a little mere the silence is enhanced and at its greatest power. It is always so in mountains, where woodland and water are combined.

Those native to the flat lands find the same thing, they say, beside the reeds of their own lakes and marshes; but I doubt whether any save those native to them would find it so. The waters of Lincolnshire had this effect upon Tennyson, who has well recorded it. I can understand that effect also in Southern Sweden and in Finland. But is it not always deeply tinged with melancholy? Does it ever give full satisfaction and repose? It is rather upon the heights where glimpses between the great trunks of the mountain pinewoods present the world below you as something remote and make you happily master of it from above that satisfy the mind.

Perhaps the Lebanon gave all this to men in its day,

though it hardly does so now. Two thousand years ago the complaint was well established that man had denuded those mountains and that their trees were murdered. Today there is little left of the famous and sacred cedars. I heard there was a grove remaining of some startlingly small number. Was it not "seventeen trees," or something of that kind? And the walls of the inner valley, now half-ruined and fallen to stagnant marshes, the empty world through which run the Orontes northward and southward the Litany, carry no true forests upon their sides. Nor is there forest upon the farther eastern wall. Would there were; for to look out upon the desert beyond Damascus from the shade and seclusion of great trees would be a contrast indeed. But if ever it were there, today this contrast has disappeared.

Will the woods return? That is the question one asks of everything which man has misused in dealing with his habitation. Those learned in the matter tell one that once the woodlands have been cut down the soil gets washed away and Nature does not replant. Man can do so. When the more patient men return by conquest to what careless men have ruined, they replant; but with difficulty, for there is no immediate gain. Hence it is that in North Africa where the greatest work of this kind has been attempted, it has, upon the whole, failed.

The Northern Peace

WE TALK OF THE NORTHERN LIGHTS AS SOMETHING peculiar to the lands up above ourselves towards the Pole and belonging to skies strange in our experience. But one does not hear, to my knowledge, the phrase "the Northern peace," yet that is a phrase which I think would be even more characteristic of all that distant land, especially of its extreme: of the ultimate Thule.

For the feeling that haunts my memory when I return to the vision I had of Scandinavia as a very young man, when I visited Sweden to its extreme north near the iron mines and sailed the whole length of the Baltic, is a feeling of profound peace: such a peace as I had not enjoyed elsewhere in Christendom: not even in the high mountains of more Southern lands.

I found everywhere not only a sort of spiritual harmony between the citizens of all these lesser countries from the Dane-work to the Arctic sea, not only the inward peace upon which all depends, but an outer condition of silence and Nature undisturbed, even undisturbed for the most part by Man. I can believe that one who should have sufficiently provisioned himself and gone on foot through the great woods of Scandinavia until he came to the more barren soil of its last Northern edges was more fully at peace with Nature around, in those distant days which lasted to the very eve of our present catastrophes, than in any other Christian countryside. Political peace had been achieved as well as the spiritual peace upon which it was founded, and the whole was bathed in an air of peace, physical and ambient as though a man were living in a calm evening that did not end.

Indeed, I call to mind one particular experience which is still as vividly before me as when I first came upon it all those forty-odd years ago. It was in the late summer, too long after the solstice for the Midnight Sun to appear, although I was in the very high North and just beyond the Arctic circle. Those colours, that glory which we connect with sunset and which are one of the chief gifts of Nature to Man in our own climate, were apparent in that night (for it was night by my watch though full day for reading and walking); only they did not lie in the West as they do with us when the sun has set but rather in the North itself, forming a sort of band, transfigured along the sky immediately above the rim of the world, behind which the sun had dipped for that very brief interval which is never night but only an introduction of a new day. A Roman writer of 2,000 years ago, who had never seen these places but who had heard them described, put it well enough when he said that even at night in that far land the sun extended its influence beyond the corners of the world. It has sometimes seemed strange to me that the more vivid consciousness of human immortality should have arisen among the Gauls rather than here in the immense silence of the North filled with, not hours, but days and weeks of continuous light.

I was vigorous enough in those days, and I walked on through the narrow forest path among the small trees till midnight (which was not midnight but only the turn of the hours) was passed. Those sunset colours continued in their magic and their multitude on until the beginning of the dawn. Nor shall I ever forget the first sharp, sudden spot of brilliance which was the very edge of the sun peeping up in a small bead of intense light through the wooded horizon: for there was no mist. From that hour onward, until the need for sleep fell upon me, the day so broadened that in another latitude I might have thought it mid-morning.

What is more, and what is odd, the air was not cold. I had read of this curious warmth with which those long days fill even the Arctic air, I had expected it from my reading, but now that I had come upon it in action, as it were, I was still surprised. And here is another note about that place and that hour. The water of the marshy stream which lay along the path I followed was warm to the hand. It was warmer even than the warm air. The long day-light and the unclouded sun reigning without interruption had done this.

This, then, was the gift given me by this journey of mine in the North so long ago. It was the chief gift, was this abiding memory of a vast peace; and when, not much over a year ago, I returned to Scandinavia I enjoyed for a moment, though I was far to the south and only on the fringes of the great forests and the mountains which are the splendour of the middle land, when I heard once more the waters and their falls and looked again upon the wide level meres, that almost violent impression of Peace returned. Those countrysides extend so endlessly, they are so happily sparse in population, and their towns and vil-lages set within such surroundings are so much at ease with the created world inanimate, they are so clothed with interminable woodland and so dominated by the ever-present silence, that there still returns to me as I call them to mind that phrase of which they seemed to me the physical expression: "The Northern Peace."

To think that war should ever fall upon such a land! Of all the lands of Europe these had seemed the most remote and the most immune from the crimes and follies of men and from the chaos of arms! Everywhere men must contrast with tragic feeling the old peace and what has now befallen; nowhere, I think, shall the few spectators of the scene (they may later be a multitude) more feel the shock of incongruity between war and peace than in these Scandinavian woodlands and high hills, deep inlets precipitous, falling into the depths of the sea, and summer snows on the high hills against the sky.

Fiords

Since fiords were in the news at the moment in which I first wrote this—the middle of April, 1940—let me consider them here. They are found on special coasts of their own: Scandinavia and New Zealand, for instance, and in south-western Ireland.

Their characteristic is that they are long and narrow inlets whereby the sea penetrates to the very heart of the land. I take it that a fiord must always be something of the kind, for we have adopted the name from Scandinavian fiords. We also associate the word with especially deep water, because most of the Scandinavian fiords, if not all of them, have that mark. We further associate them commonly, but not universally, with very high banks on either side, often rising to precipitous cliffs and standing before a background of mountain.

Now I take it that the character of the fiord in history has been determined by these two things. First, its excellence as harbour and next, the ease of its defence, especially before the development of very long-range artillery—in which we must include aircraft: for aircraft as used for attack is essentially a form of long-range artillery. The excellence of the fiord as a harbour is obvious from the depth of its water and the way in which any narrow inlet of sufficient length creates between its banks a strip of calm protected water. The only exception to this is when a valley of this kind runs quite straight from the sea inwards and broadens fairly rapidly towards its mouth, and such formations are rare.

Most fiords ramify, and nearly all of them have bends between their upper reaches and the open sea. Even the fiord of Morlaix in Brittany, which is a good example of a straight approach for miles into the heart of the land, has a crook at the end of it which shelters it from the north wind. If you look at the plan of any one of the Norwegian fiords you will be astonished at the complexity of the waterway. This holds also of the prolonged inlets which separate the Danish islands and bear locally the name of fiord. The most remarkable of these is the narrow belt of salt water expanding to a sort of lake in the central part; I mean the Lim Fiord on which Aalborg stands, and which cuts off the extreme north of Jutland making an island of it. This extraordinary piece of water goes twisting about from the Kattegat all the way to the North Sea at the western end; salt water all the way and yet, for the most part, no broader than a minor river and particularly narrow at either end: a natural training ground for boatmen. There are, I suppose, seventy miles at least between the two entrances: counting all the twists and turns in the main channel, perhaps another five or seven. I ought by rights to get out my maps and measure it for you, but I am too lazy. Also I ought to look up the derivation of the word "fiord," but to do that would be to pretend to a language which I do not possess, so I will let it go.

What we may call the true fiord, the deep, narrow, mountainous, drowned valley of sea-water, I have called an excellent harbour because of its calm water and its uncommonly great depth. But the latter point sometimes interferes with the finding of an anchorage. The shores are often steep too and that, by the way, has been a cause of difficulty in finding ships which had taken refuge in the fiords or were preparing to issue therefrom. Even air reconnaissance has sometimes been baffled, for the cliffs hide a ship until the plane is right over it. In this character of theirs as good harbours there occurs a curious point which I have never seen explained, nor even often written about: and this is that *just the districts that most seem to need harbours most lack them, and just the districts that are most plentifully supplied with harbours lack the inland districts at their back which could put those harbours to use.*

Look at the innumerable natural harbours of the eastern Adriatic coast and note that the countrysides to which they give access have not much developed agriculture and no industries. On the western side of that sea, where there is a fertile belt hundreds of miles long and many first-rate towns, there are very few harbours. Brindisi is, indeed, a remarkable natural harbour on the extreme south; and Venice, with its sheltered lagoons and delta islands, the obvious natural opportunity on the extreme north. But in between you only have Ancona, which is no natural harbour but only a crook in the land. It is not a general rule, but it is a strangely common one, that natural harbours stand where they are not wanted and are ironically absent from shores where they are wanted.

What they lack in economic value the fiords as a rule make up in beauty, which is, I suppose, more important than anything economic, though you can't live on it; a truth which all poets have discovered—usually, rather late in their lives.

Of course, you only get this quality of natural beauty, what is called "picturesque," where the fiords lie in mountainous land. That is what so much the greater part of them do. It would be a fine argument with which to tease the economic or the materialist interpreters of history to put forward the thesis that fiords were created by way of compensation as though the makers of them had said, "I can't provide you with goods, but I can make it up with loveliness." The thesis would not hold water (unlike the fiord, by the way, whose whole point is holding water), but, as I say, it would make a very good text for ragging the intellectuals; it would make an even better text than the teleological views of the past generation.

And talking of those views, does anyone still remember, I wonder, Ambrose Bierce's fable of the elephant and the giraffe? The giraffe praised God for its long neck which enabled it to get at the tender leaves of the higher branches and told the elephant he ought to feel the same gratitude (seeing that his neck was not there) for his long trunk. To which the elephant replied, "I see you have been among the theologians."

Stockholm Remembered

I HAVE WRITTEN ON STOCKHOLM MORE THAN ONCE BEFORE now; so I ask to be excused for it. It is a town, the image of which changed in my mind during the interval of years between my first and my second visiting it. When I first saw it, it seemed to me more beautiful than it did when I saw it the second time. But I daresay the change was in myself (dear Brutus) and not in Stockholm. Also in the interval there had come certain modern buildings of the sort which moderns admire and which I do not: but here let me say as amply as I can that no man can be a fixed judge of these things. A man may judge rightly indeed of any work of art which greatly pleases him; but on what displeases him, if it pleases others as worthy as himself, he has no right to make too sure. It reminds one of what people say about a marriage, "What can he have seen in her?" Well, at any rate he saw it, and that is good enough for him.

What I have in common to all my memories of Stockholm is the dignity and ubiquity of the calm Swedish water which gives its note to all that land. Stockholm is essentially the city of a lake and of lakes. All Sweden is a land of lakes wherein are mirrored innumerable miles of repeated trees, and into which and from which flow innumerable broad calm rivers. Stockholm is, perhaps, more full of history than any other of the lesser capitals in

Europe, and that is because those who took the throne in the turbulent moment of the sixteenth century were warriors.

The Vasa family had something about it which made for history; so that in either branch, orthodox and traditional, convert or rebel, legitimate heir or usurper, every Vasa stamped himself upon his time. I know of few more striking contrasts in travel than to look upon the statue of the sacred Vasa on his column in Warsaw (I hope the wars have left it intact) and then beyond the intervening sea, upon the statue of that other Vasa—full of a vigorous advance, somewhat insolent: a man, commanding troops— which stands in the little square near his old palace, which he and his family made the capital of Sweden. It is right, I think, that the palace on its small particular island, should dominate the city as it does. Not that it stands upon a height or that it has pinnacles or towers; it is a level thing and in the classical tradition; but it is representative of something great; a lineage which summed up in itself a whole people.

The popular tags about famous sites and cities seem to me as a rule to miss the mark; and whoever invented the phrase about Stockholm, which calls it "the Venice of the North," seems to me, upon reflection, to have got things wrong. The only thing Stockholm has in common with Venice is that both are water towns, unless we add that both are harbours, inland and sheltered, and both of them have been or are the heads of States. Venice is a name which might be taken for the symbol of the serene and the superb. Venice is queenly, Stockholm is homely: Venice is full of colour, indeed the spirit of colour informs the whole place and made its artistic story; you cannot think of Venice without thinking at once of all her colours, from the mosaics to Titian and from the glorious brick to the reflected palace walls in her lagoons. Also Venice was queenly in ruling and (what is a minor point) marvellous in wealth.

I call that a minor point, because to exaggerate the value of wealth in the story of a city is an error only less than to exaggerate it in the story of a man. But when it has been present it should be remembered, for wealth (as the philosopher said—and he delighted, as you know, in the obvious and commonplace) purchases many things. It purchased for Venice such splendid shipping, such porticoes and such pictures as no city ever had before, or has since combined. But there was something much more than her wealth in Venice. There was some spirit or other which glowed through it all and now still shines with an undying flame.

Not so Stockholm. The beauty of Stockholm, where you get it, is from without. The city is remembered years after the traveller has left it; but remembered less for its content or for its monuments than for the nature around it. As your ship moves away from Venice, you look back on a distant vision of splendour, man-made and a triumph for man. As your ship moves away from Stockholm, you look back upon something grey which mixes with undistinguished hills around.

Nevertheless, Stockholm contains this secret of the north, *mystery;* Stockholm has produced in the past and will, I think, recover in the future, legends or episodes which touch on things beyond the world—but things of the night: winter things.

That story which has moved me most in the long record of the city (I have described it elsewhere) is the story of the Hand.

It will be remembered that Fersen, the devoted lover of Marie Antoinette, the devoted lover and nothing more, was murdered years after that great episode in his life by the mob in a political fury, acting as mobs do rather like beasts than men. He was already elderly. His mind was furnished with nothing but one great memory of a poignant ineradicable sort, which belonged to his youth. He was still in the thirties when he drove the Queen and her husband and their children out of Paris in the flight to Varennes. Two years after, her head had fallen upon the scaffold and he has left on record a sort of shriek with which he met the news. He loved her with all his heart and she loved him.

That, I say, was in his thirties. He was in his fifties when the angry fools tore him to pieces in their folly. That night his severed hand, set up on the prow of a boat, is said to have shone with a miraculous light and to have directed the boatmen to a goal preordained, pointing the way. It may only be a myth, but there was some such profound emotion creating the myth as has made it permanent. And false or true the relation is thoroughly Scandinavian. It is in tune with those visions of things beyond the world and things not of the holier sort with which stories of those woods, those streams, those hills are full.

Scandinavian Sculpture

The North—I mean Sweden and Denmark—has for now more than a hundred years made itself famous in sculpture and this Scandinavian stream of talent—now and then genius—does not dry up.

I had known this (as men know things through print) all my life, but I *realised* it in quite a new way when I crossed over a few months ago to see Denmark and Sweden, to revisit them after forty years—more than forty years. I suppose that a place which has been known in the past and unvisited for so long, strikes one even more freshly than if it were new, and there was of course a great deal of stuff which in my first voyage either was not yet there or had not been noticed by me. I have no qualifications for criticising any form of art. I do no more than speak as I am moved to speak by a certain enthusiasm in discovery, including the discovery of much that is old and which I ought to have known before.

There has appeared, then, somewhat suddenly in quite modern times a body of remarkable work, and the first question a modern man will ask of such a phenomenon is, "Why in this place, and why at this time?" Why did Scandinavia come to the forefront in this art, which we had all associated with another climate of Europe, and with another political tradition?

Such questions arise continually in the history of art; indeed, save for the great monuments of high antiquity, before the perfection of the Greeks, one may say that all plastic art and particularly sculpture appears in this fashion, spasmodically, as it were, sprouting in a special field, luxuriant in that field, perfected at the best—or at the worst full of energy, and then turns into something other and less, or even disappears. It was so with the marvellous statuary of the late twelfth and still more of the thirteenth century, adorning anonymously the Gothic cathedrals of the West. It was so with that astonishing chapter, the human portraiture of the Dutch in the seventeenth century. It is so in Scandinavia today, from the early nineteenth century onwards.

There is no answer to the questions proposed. The efforts made to explain these things historically never satisfy the inquirer. There is as a rule, an original outbreak, as it were, of creation, a longer or shorter period of increasing excellence and then the change; often the death. One cannot say that Scandinavia enjoyed any special tradition to make it do in these things what it has done. One certainly cannot say that climatic conditions account for it in any way; and for my part I do not think that any racial theory in this field is valid. The thing happens. Why it happens, and the limits to which it is confined in space and time are beyond our solution.

It is true that Scandinavia had, right away from the beginning, from the pagan time, an unfailing spring of energy in this matter, the famous barbaric stone at Jelling is an example. But why that energy flowered so late, and when it did, we cannot say.

As things now stand, the sculpture of Denmark and Sweden has not struck home, but at the origin of its modern fame it bears the great name of Thorwaldsen. It is the twin name in the North to that of Canova in the South, and both Thorwaldsen and Canova had this in common: a sort of unlively perfection which gave them in their own time what is not unjustly called an exaggerated fame. Patriotism will read into the work of the first some specially northern quality, some peculiarly Scandinavian character; but I doubt whether that reading is real. I doubt whether, if you were to put a piece of the great Dane's best work before a man who had never heard of it he would say, "This is Northern." It is not of a climate or of blood, it is simply the effort, and the successful effort, to create after a tradition which the man found elsewhere—unless creation be too strong a word. But at any rate, Thorwaldsen is an opening and a gate so far as the renown of his country in this art is concerned.

For my own part, I do not feel life in him, save (perhaps oddly) in the two famous medallions called, I think, *Night* and *Morning*. There is in these a sort of arrested grace, of progressive movement, which is living enough. But for the rest, it seems to be with him, as with Canova, that there was no inward flame.

Yet Thorwaldsen desired and achieved excellence. He even aimed at perfection, and within a certain technical framework himself believed that he had reached it. That was certainly believed by the men of his own time and long after him. Yet probably some distant future will rather be arrested by the vigorous personalities in stone of which I find the chief to be the great statue of Gustavus Vasa in the heart of that which he made: royal Stockholm. There is here no sentimental error that I am aware of; I confess to a certain admiration for Gustavus though none for his philosophy, if he had one, and less for his morals. But he was a leader and a soldier. He had the art of command: of that there is no doubt. And his statue is the monument of that.

Here again is a personal impression, and no more—it seemed to me as I wandered about without prejudice, looking at what were to me for the most part new things (though of some few I retained a blurred memory from the past) that the Scandinavians had at least this specifically Northern about them, that animals move them to their strongest expression. If you will look all round the group of the goddess and her oxen, you will I think feel the oxen more strongly than the goddess. It is energy at work: it is full life without extravagance. And another group which I came upon purely by chance and stood before at once, halted by good surprise, is that of the *Bull Mastering the Serpent* in front of the Town Hall at Copenhagen. It is as vital as can be! It is in the tradition, as to the one part of it, of those fine writhing dragons which curl and slide down the steeple of the old Bourse (I think it is) near the harbour. It is a thing difficult to put before the reader; it is something you must walk round and look at, from this aspect and from that. And in your memory of it, it still remains magnificently alive.

There is another tradition, also living enough and vital, but a tradition of more repose: the *Mermaid* is the most famous, I think, in that tradition in so far as it is modern, but I took for my own part a much greater pleasure in the little *Merchild* of the Public Docks, and I thought as I looked on it what a good thing it would be if men were to return for inspiration to innocence. Innocence has in it something far more profound than tortured invention, or than the search for novelty. They that get inspiration from innocence are well served. You may find that in a hundred unknown excellences of our own day, which perhaps will never be famous, but all of them have the particular quality of youth—I mean, of very early youth.

We have heard, perhaps too often, that the first work

had less vitality, the Scandinavians sought to make good by an excess of motion. Now excess of motion is never consonant to stone. It is not even consonant to bronze. It would seem that plastic art when it reproduces the human form demands what is also demanded by the reproduction of facial expression, by the portrait in bronze or in stone, or by the ideal head.

How to express this quality, I know not. It is something more than reserve. It is like an undertone of power. It is not motion arrested. It is not motion potential. It is rather that promise of the inhabiting soul which can inform something that would be otherwise dead or half-dead.

To express what I mean, I will cite the best work of Houdon, who has always seemed to me the greatest master of transferring human life to marble. But then Houdon stands by himself, not in degree but in quality.

I may be wrong. No one can affirm a universal from a particular, but I at least know of no other man who achieved that life which Houdon achieved, and which catches you, which holds you, when you are looking at the common features of a king or the profound irony of such a genius as Voltaire. I would even say that Houdon alone brings Rousseau back to us as he was, and in the shape Houdon has given Rousseau we can forgive Rousseau. A thing not always easy.

The modern Scandinavians, as it seems to me, have erred in too active a hunt for novelty.

They err in good company, for nearly all our best of the younger generation suffers from that too-active quest. Their grotesque is striking enough—too striking—but it is not the spontaneous grotesque of their ancestors. They compel one to look, they do not compel one to admire. It is true of their sculpture as it is true of their architecture. For though I know that I am here at issue with all the critics I must say the truth when I say that the famous Town Hall of Stockholm seems to me to have failed. I cannot but think that men coming after us will say, "This is no introduction to the great port: this is something not married to the rest." If a man may be allowed to praise what he himself has most enjoyed, and to do it without reference to any canon laid down by others, I would praise the accidental statuary of the Swedish and the Danish parks. It seems to me filled with the spirit of the glades in which it stands, of the quiet water which it adorns, and of the lawns against which the white stone shows so clear.

Unfortunately, it is difficult or impossible to convey the effect of this by reproduction. It is an effect of happening, or accident. You walk by the waterside, you turn a group of thicket and you find a companion. When you have passed you look back on him or her as to something you will remember as a friend.

Now this (if a foreigner may say it without impertinence) is perhaps the most notable quality of the Scandinavians in all they do, and no wonder it appears in their plastic art, particularly when that art is not too much concerned with its own fame and is half nameless through its spontaneity.

That is the quality which charmed all Europe in the literary work of Hans Christian Andersen. How typical of such work it is, the man who does it often does not know what he has done! So it was, as we all know, with Andersen. I have read that he never understood why he had become so suddenly famous. It seems that he made no effort, that he desired no renown.

The leading spiritual quality in all that is the virtue of simplicity. They had it and they will return to it. In proof of which, remark how every traveller returning from Scandinavia, and particularly from Denmark, recalls with delight the universal friendliness which enveloped him everywhere. I say the testimony to this is universal, and amply deserved.

I could wish to come back to those narrow seas and those restricted happy summers some generations hence and find that to a native simplicity, in sculpture as in letters, the North had returned, and when you think of it, what an admirable miracle it is that this quality arose, historically, from an origin of violence and barbarism.

Who worked that miracle? I know not; but I am glad that it was done.

Of Norwegian work I have said nothing because I have seen nothing. I must apologise for the omission.

Bothnia and the Finland Belt

FINLAND MEANS THE EASTERN SIDE OF THAT LARGE, BROAD, tongue-shaped sheet of water which is called the Gulf of Bothnia, and is bottle-necked by the Aaland Islands. It has been, if not exactly colonised, at any rate dominated by Scandinavian influence from the other side of the water for we know not how many generations. To-day it is in tradition, culture and religion, which lies at the root of all culture, virtually a Scandinavian country.

But the region has a geographical interest distinct from the racial and cultural tradition. Its southern part is a mass of forests, the exact copy of the unending woodlands of short pine on the western side of the sea. Its northern part is that fringe of the ultimate end of the Baltic, the shores that curl round the north-eastern, northern, and north-western shores of the gulf, and this northern part has a character of its own, somewhat different from the southern part, though one merges into the other.

The southern half of Finland is, in a more intense way, a continuation of the Swedish note, the note of lakes, boulders and rocks in an endless carpet of woodland, built up of short conifers. But southern Finland has these things in a multitude. A man flying over it (which I have not done) sees, I am told, such a mass of isolated water patches, from very large lakes to mere pools, that the thing looks under a morning summer sun like torn and ragged lace, supposing such lace to be green in colour and stretched over a shining surface of mirror.

In the northern half you get hills inland, I am told, but even greater isolation of territory than in the south. Then, in the extreme north, you get what I suppose may fairly be called an extension of the Tundra: that is, very unfertile land with all vegetation, including trees and bushes, thoroughly stunted. All that northern edge of the old world is inhuman, unintended for men. Round the corner, when you get towards the last effect of the Atlantic, there is warmer water and the headlands are bolder. But the thing is still arctic, though the harbours do not freeze as they do to the east of the projection. It is said that the "swish of warm water" (which begins far south by being called the Gulf Stream) is accountable for that odd northern extension of the Isotherms. It may be so. I leave that to my betters.

The part which I know best of all this land is the inner edge of the Gulf of Bothnia, whither I arrived and whence I departed with a companion of my own age, much the better part of a lifetime ago. It was in the high summer of 1895, but somewhat after the longest day, that we set out on this adventure. I have always retained vivid memories of it, though very little happened, for completely new skies, a completely new earth, new landscapes, a new air are sufficient adventure for anyone, and will always be remembered.

Let me here do what I have done in the matter of most of my journeys, that is, set down the things that struck me immediately and almost violently at the time. There was the endless daylight, just as, at this season, the endless darkness. The sunset lay along the northern horizon and the dawn became part of it long before it had time to cast shadows.

Then there were the mosquitoes. I believe that they are common to all the arctic shore, and they are certainly a hellish marvel!

It has been said by a wise man that the really astonishing things of this world are hardly ever emphasised. That is certainly true of Portland race and of the very rare miracles of good poetry. It is also true of saintly people, but it is especially true of the mosquitoes of the arctic.

They are incredible, for number, for activity, and for ubiquity. They must be seen and felt to be believed. Certain writers have done them justice, particularly the late Lord Dufferin, who wrote on all this part of the world as lively a book as you may care to read. Indeed, I know that dozens of travellers have talked about the mosquitoes of the North, but they have not got over the footlights, though they are as truly remarkable of Canadian high latitudes (I am told) as of Scandinavian or Russian—and no doubt of Asiatic Russia as well.

Then I remember this. That in such an unnatural summer light the water of the many tumultuous streams never got cold. I suppose in the corresponding winter darkness it never loses bite even when it does not freeze. And another thing I remember is the careful garnering of sustenance for man and beast in that inhospitable land: the tiny pyramids of coarse hay wrapped round standard poles in dwarf ricks. The strangely thin spread of oats in the few places where oats would grow. Whether they had fruit I know not; I came across none. Of human habitation there was very little indeed.

When my companion and I had wandered about as long as we dared (for we knew that we must get back south to Lulea before our money gave out lest we should never see dear England again), we turned back towards the shores of the Gulf, and as we approached Lulea we saw yet another thing not to be forgotten. It was an enormous flag streaming in the breeze bearing the inscription "Lulea for Christ." (I believe one ought to make a sort of little circle or something over the "a" of Lulea, but I cannot go into all that. Our fathers never bothered about spelling, and they were greater than we.)

Well, when we had got to the water again and the human stir of Lulea town and harbour, what happened to us? We were arrested: neither for the first nor the last time in our lives. For we had known that adventure in the University town of Oxford on occasions of especial glory, and I was to know it again in many another place: it is a common happening to wandering men.

He who arrested us was a magnificent man. He might have served as a type of advertisement of what people mean by "Nordic." Whether his muscles were strong I doubt, for in that matter your blond giant of the all-conquering race is sometimes a little disappointing. But at any rate he would have photographed magnificently. He cross-examined us closely on the hypothesis that we were American criminals, whereas we were as blameless as the Ethiopians. At last he discharged us from custody, but with the caution that we should be watched.

When we were free we bargained with a ship-captain (who was taking a cargo of iron-ore) to carry us to some north-sea port. He said he was going to the Humber, but he stuck in the fairway. There are no tides up there. High-water only means an exceptional relay from the summer melting of the ice. It had not proved quite enough, and so, what with the delay, by the time we were disembarked on Lulea quay again, almost the last of our money was gone. We bargained with a kindly and elderly bearded German who was taking a cargo of wood into the Scheldt to take us thither, saying we would work our passage by helping to shift the high-piled planks when such labour was needed. After some days of calm churning through the Baltic flat and a very violent night or two between the Belt and the Scheldt, we were landed on Dutch quays.

During the last lap of our odd exploration there came yet another experience which has stuck in my mind. Well before we got to the Aaland Islands (which are a swarm of rocks like a swarm of mosquitoes, and were, perhaps, inspired by those insects) a deck-hand who could speak a little English asked me whether I knew that the water of the gulf was fresh? I said I did not know it. I had thought it to be part of the salt sea. Then, to prove his words, he made a sort of cradle for a tumbler out of string and lowered it over the side and bade me drink. And lo! it was as fresh as the water of any warm ditch in my own dear county!

Thus as I wandered did I learn new things.

The Vistula and Thorn

I HAD OCCASION SOME YEARS AGO, AFTER THE LIBERATION OF
Poland but before the first new movement among the Germans, to travel down the Vistula from Warsaw to the
neighbourhood of Danzig.

It is an experience I have heard compared to a journey
down the Mississippi; but though I have said before now
how much the banks of the Vistula at Warsaw, the bridges
and the houses nearby, reminded me of Western America,
there is no close parallel between the aspect of the Vistula
as a river and the aspect of the Mississippi. The Vistula is
a much more regularly bounded stream until you get to
the neighbourhood of its Delta. There are few marshy belts
on either approach to the main water. On the Mississippi
these are continually appearing. The crossings of that enormous flood have a sort of tentative character, as though the
railway were trying the temperature of the water with its
toes before going right in. It is often difficult to say where
the true river begins; and the Mississippi swirls and changes
its bed continually, a thing you do not see (or at least I
did not see it) on the Polish river. The Vistula is altogether
more defined and neat and, though it is very broad and
therefore somewhat shallow for its volume, it is not nearly
so broad as even the Upper Mississippi and the shoals seem
less capricious and less numerous.

The steamer that took me down the Vistula was built for

shallow water, and what interested me most about it was its method of accosting the banks in the course of its journey. Where there was wharfage and a fairly good draft of water alongside the landing-place the boat would draw up and moor; but in most other places it behaved in a fashion I have never seen anywhere else. It would run its nose into the mud of the bank, so that there would be a gap between the prow and the hard shore. A sort of gangway was run out from the prow to the dry land, and the people who wanted to get off walked precariously along it. Then, when the last passenger was off, the gangway plank was shipped aboard again and the boat made great efforts (always *at last* successful!) to back away from the bank and find herself again in water deep enough to float her. She reversed engines, turning until she had succeeded in pulling herself free, lashing up a great foam, and making one wonder which would win in this tug of war.

As I went on down the Vistula I noticed the way in which, in one place after another, careful cultivation came right down to the water's edge, neat gardens, and how the riverside towns, which were at some distance one from another, used as a platform for their architecture and a setting for their individuality the low bluffs on which they were built. It was their antiquity which gave them this advantage. For, all over Europe townships and villages with a long past behind them marry thus into the landscape; it is only our modern industrial civilisation that has no instinct for harmony between the soil and the habitations of men.

I remember one little town especially (though I have forgotten its name) which stood above the waters and mirrored itself therein as neatly as something on the stage, and, for my part, I find nothing more satisfactory in travel than places which remind me of the Opera, with the added advantage that there is no blaring music.

Of all the towns I came on during this river voyage of mine down the Vistula the one that struck me most was Thorn. Thorn is the Western name for it, the alien German form. The native, Polish, name is Torun. It seemed to me the most national thing, after Cracow, that I had come upon this journey. Perhaps Thorn has caught this special imprint through reaction against the Prussian domination which overshadowed it for two long lifetimes and more. The Prussian rule over that part of Poland, including the lower Vistula, which had been imposed in the partitions, was more odious to those subjected to it than was even the Tsarist domination higher up in the mid-part of the river's course. This alien spirit was the more evident from the fact that all the big modern buildings were affected by it, from the ungainly big railway station downwards. The houses of the town, which had tradition and were national, had also grace and beauty; but the central and best thing in the town was its cathedral, alive with the ancient religion by which Poland lived and lives.

Almost under the shadow of that cathedral is the statue of the man who has made Thorn most famous in foreign ears. I mean the statue of Copernicus, for Copernicus was of Thorn.

Today, since men are wild with nationalism, they will angrily debate whether Copernicus was Polish or German. He had German blood certainly, but as certainly he was a Pole, and still more certainly neither he himself nor his contemporaries troubled as we do today about such matters as race and blood. There was always, as people are never tired of telling us, *some* contrast between the Teuton and the Slav, but the contrast which people cared for a great deal more than that was the contrast in general culture and religion. This man who, by his hypothesis and his efforts at demonstrating its truth, changed man's view upon man's own earthly habitation, was not the first to propound the conception of a solar system, still less was he the first to conceive the mobility of the globe. But he came just at that moment of change and expansion in all external experience which allowed the new idea to catch on and which fostered it.

Copernicus was the elder contemporary of Calvin—thirty-four years older, but he survived to hear the renown of Calvin's work. He overlapped the beginnings of that revolution and turmoil in everything which marked the first generation of the sixteenth century. The treatise by which we remember him was finished in 1530, though you first find it printed, I believe, ten years later: and it was not until 1543 that the complete exposition appeared under the title by which we now know it, just in time for Copernicus himself to see it as he was dying. I would like to know (but no one will ever know) what place he gave in his own mind to this one of his very many labours. For he was a churchman, a mathematician, a teacher, and many other things. Certainly he did not know that anything so simple, so imperfect, and so unconnected with the essential questions of life would be made a battleground well within a century of its appearance.

On the pedestal of his statue there is written a Latin phrase which best describes what he did: "He moved the earth and he made the sun stand still."

Not only Thorn, but Cracow, can boast Copernicus. His life belongs to all the Vistula, or rather his achievements do; for he lived here and there. It was the University of Cracow which taught him what he knew and gave him speculation, though it was perhaps his journey to Italy, where he heard so much adverse discussion of the old classical astronomy, that started him on his new road. It is singular and a great blessing that the mind which thus prepared such violent controversies should itself have been fairly free from quarrels. The Copernican teaching slipped in easily enough among the theories of its own time, causing at first no strains and no angers, and breeding very little fame. There are not many men who stand at the origin of any great change and yet are free from the pangs of creation and the heavy task of transforming the concepts of men and forcing them into line with reality. He was so blessed.

Danzig

DANZIG HAS THIS IN COMMON WITH A GREAT MANY
medieval towns of Europe: that it has a wonderful *old*
town and a common, tawdry, modern extension outside
that nucleus.

In all such cities you are seized by the sharp contrast between the days when civilisation was still more or less
united and still had a sense of beauty, and the ethical and
aesthetic chaos that followed and swamped our world.

The old town of Danzig, that which originally lay
within the walls of that famous port, is as beautiful as anything I have seen. Its principal broad but long Market
Place, leading to the Water Gate, and so to the wharves of
the old harbour, distantly reminds one of the splendid
Municipal Square in Brussels, a glory of the late Renaissance; and the reason that one is reminded of Brussels, so
many hundred miles away, is that here in Danzig you get
a last effect of that which most travelling men first find in
Brussels—I mean stone-gilt. The transition between the
Middle Ages and later times discovered, and used in Flanders and Brabant, this noble form of decoration. I know
of no parallel to it outside those merchant towns of the
North. The grey elaborately carven stone is picked out
everywhere with gilding, and the gilding marries with the
colour of the stone astonishingly.

Another thing which struck me very much in my walks

through that most famous of the cities of the Southern Baltic shore was the way in which it exemplifies the rôle of the old European harbour and the contrast between the former and the modern use.

Water carriage had the supreme advantage of cheapness over land carriage; and this advantage was especially emphasised in the days before modern road making, especially in the days before the railway. You could take by water, from the first port for as many miles up country as the draught would serve, in one container—as the cargo of one barge—material which would have needed special loading on a hundred carts at least; and the road was a manner of transport only to be used by day and ruinously expensive in labour. I have never seen calculated the probable comparative cost of carrying, say, fifty tons of goods by water and by road per mile in those days, but the co-efficient, whatever it may have been, is sure to be very large.

Danzig, standing on the best navigable branch of the Vistula delta, was the gate of water carriage for hundreds of miles inland. That central fluvial backbone of the Polish plains was the creator of Danzig and the support thereof, for the whole meaning of Danzig was that it was the Vistula gate of Poland, the *one* port of Poland opening on to the outer world.

Yet it was not a Polish city in the ethnical sense or the cultural. It was and is a German city, in speech, in social habit, in everything. But its traditions were not rooted in any idea of German unity. It was like the other Hanseatic towns, one individual unit separate from the rest, not even a link in a chain, but an island in an archipelago. One need not, in order to explain Danzig, in order to apprehend this German gate of the vast Polish field, weave fantastic theories about a Teutonic race, more adventurous than, and thus superior to, its neighbours. The cause is simpler than that, and obvious enough historically. Civilisation came to the Northern Germans earlier than it came to the tribes of the Southern Baltic littoral. The German culture, in its early medieval origins, could found a commercial town and exploit its possibilities among populations which had as yet no European life or traditions; and that is why the South Baltic ports were all Germanic at root, while the countrysides around them, up to their very walls, were Slavonic. The towns already had the culture of Christendom when the things around them were pagan. This lead they never lost.

Another mark of most old medieval ports is the (to our eyes) exiguity of the waterway. It is not everywhere so. Antwerp has for a whole day's sailing up to it a splendid crescent of very broad deep water, and everyone knows the size and dignity of the Thames below bridges and the nobility of the river at London. But in Danzig, as in fifty other cases, it was a comparatively small and narrow waterway which brought in sea-borne traffic, a winding and difficult river nowhere of great depth: for remember that this was but a delta branch of the Vistula, and not the main stream.
Danzig had not the advantage of a tide; that force which carries heavy burdens to and fro without human aid was lacking to the port. Nor, so far as I know, was Danzig, as London was, the lowest bridge, and therefore the natural place of transhipment. But in general Danzig was created by and served the same purposes as London. It received all that came in by the salt (or rather brackish) Baltic water outside; it distributed those cargoes up the inland plains by way of the river at the mouth of which it stood guardian.
With the political decline of Poland, Danzig, which is bound up with the fortunes of Poland, could not but de-

cline. When the last partition came in the late eighteenth century, the main market of Danzig was gone. The town acquired that special note of calm and age which is the benediction of all dying cities and of most economic decay. Such an afterglow lit the streets of Rome within the memory of men and women still living; some tradition of it still lingers in Danzig.

Even to-day Danzig is not a busy place nor a noisy one, in spite of its new docks. It is in full tradition with its own past, and wise men (including its own wise men) will, I think, hope that it shall always so remain. When I saw it, Gdynia, its rival, was as modern as a port can be: made at one stroke, with the resources of modern capital and modern machinery, wonderfully efficient, springing up out of nothing into a town of myriads over night, as it were. There was perhaps no more violent contrast in Europe than the contrast between those twin closely neighboring maritime cities, disputing (or rather halving by arrangement) the whole of the maritime trade, entry and exit, from the vast continental area of Poland.

But remember this: that not even with indefinitely large expenditure could you make Danzig a modern port, any more than you could make Central London a modern port, whereas Gdynia may expand indefinitely—may accommodate when it will, if it be so compelled, the whole trade of Poland. That economic fact is food for thought.

Warsaw Remembered

I WAS SAYING SOME TIME AGO, WHEN I WROTE ON A DISTANT memory of Moscow, that the statement of visual impressions, however trivial, was of chief value in any reminiscence of actual experience; and I would apply that rule today to the case of Warsaw.

I first saw Warsaw in the late summer of 1912 in that same centenary year when I went eastward to study the campaign of Napoleon. I have revisited the town twice since then, last time after the liberation of Poland, and as the capital of a free nation. But the first impression of a foreign city is usually the keenest, and so it is in my case with Warsaw. It is my visit in 1912 which stands out most vividly in my mind, though blurred with the passage of nearly thirty years. I had come straight through from Berlin, and the contrast will always stay fixed in my mind.

The first thing that struck me was that I had come into the air of the eighteenth century out of the mechanised and spiritually sterile early twentieth. The architecture of the palaces and greater noble houses, the details of ornament, the portraits and the carvings were of the French influence, as it was in the last generations of the *ancien régime*. They had the grace and the beauty of that time and a strong savour of our Western culture, of which Warsaw, on this first sight of it, seemed, after Berlin, at once a good relic and an outpost. All this was embedded, of course, in a background of earlier things.

The churches rather recalled Vienna, so did many of the lesser private buildings. The clerical building especially was of the "Rococo," which was, in my youth, too much despised, but has lately been in part re-established and well defended, especially in the work of Mr. Sitwell. Here the effect of the later counter reformation was very apparent. The style is often called "Jesuit" on account of the influence of the Jesuits on church life during the early and mid-eighteenth century before the suppression of the Order. The term is not inappropriate. The buildings to which it refers are the more impressed with Western influence on account of that strong religious counterattack which marked the time. But of later eighteenth-century spirit in the clerical architecture I remember very little. No doubt it is amply present, but it has not remained in my mind. It is rather in the domestic, and especially the palatial, buildings, as I have said, that the air of the old régime of France in its last phase is felt.

Behind all this there is yet another background which appears most strongly in the older and central part of the city, especially in what I remember of its old square or market place, in the midst of which stands the statue of the Vasa King, who presided over the re-establishment of the State after the violent divisions of the Reformation period.

It is true that these divisions never reached the bulk of the people. They were hardly known to the peasantry, who still form the mass of the Polish population and who, in those days, formed nearly the whole of it. It was the moment when Warsaw itself began for the first time to be the capital of Poland, a part it was fitted to play from its central situation and more easy transport by water at a point where the Vistula was already broad and fairly deep.

This was never true of Cracow, the old sacred capital of the Poles. I do not know how far the influence of Warsaw as a capital spread among the Polish people. One could not help a feeling that there was something less rooted about it than there was about Cracow. Cracow also had its University tradition, which was very powerful, though it later fell into decay.

But, so far as the superficial observation of a foreigner goes, one cannot but believe that Warsaw, as capital, gathered to itself under modern conditions, not only the main political, but the main cultural springs of Polish life. For it was bound after the Industrial Revolution to be the place where the chief newspapers would be printed and to be the main and nodal point of national communications.

Warsaw was, however, badly maimed in the part it had to play as a national centre by the partitions.

It was, geographically, and in every other way, the centre of the Russian domination, but the Eastern Provinces, the character of which centred rather in the town of Poznan (or Posen), were much more highly developed on the material side, especially after the coming of machinery. There was a far more efficient and widespread road system, and contacts of all kinds were more rapid and secure on the western than on the eastern side of that artificial line which had been drawn between the Russian and the Prussian domination after the last partition, confirmed on the defeat of Napoleon, and rendered, as it seemed at the time, permanent by two long lifetimes of continued alien rule. The partition was completed some few years before and during the French Revolution. The modern Poland, restored to life by the victory of the Allies twenty years ago, did wonders in uniting the communications and other consolidating elements in the country: but the rule of the invader and despoiler had left a deep mark.

There was in the midst of Warsaw when I first came there in 1912 a most remarkable outward and visible symbol of such alien rule. In the midst of an open place, central to the life of the city, stood a huge and brand-new Russian cathedral, with everything about it utterly un-Polish. It was like a seal of conquest stamped upon a people who had continuously and vigorously risen to recover their freedom, but so far had failed.

It was as startling and as shocking a thing as would be a modern French ecclesiastical building of the largest size, glaringly modern and filled with the Liturgy of an alien religion, set up in the midst of the City of London.

That monument has since been destroyed, as complete disappearance was one of the first tasks of the new Poland. For when I came again to the city, after the passage of not a dozen years, the big empty space, levelled and without even rubble upon it, where the vast new Russian cathedral had stood, was an exact example of the Biblical phrase, "There shall not be left of it a stone upon a stone."

A further element in the dissipation of the influence of Warsaw had been the Southern Polish belt taken over by Austria. Here the alien influence had come much later and had been much milder. It is not putting it too violently to say that the resurrection of Poland after the Great War was a spirit moving northward from the Holy City of the Polish kings.

Warsaw, like every modern capital, had vastly increased in size as an effect of the industrial revolution which transformed all our lives, even here, to the east of the continent.

That influence had not too much affected the ancient beauties of the place. Warsaw was not, as Lodz became, a mere welter of industrialism, iron and modern brick and smoke, but it expanded out of all knowledge, and one very sharp reminder of the change which mechanical production had brought was the huge iron bridge over the Vistula, to-day, I suppose, blown up.

That girder bridge, stretching from one high bank to the other, added to the odd "Western America" feeling which this riverside of the ancient town gave me. It was probably an illusion due to the way in which the newcomer sees most intensely the larger and more modern thing thrust upon his sight. But it was due also, I think, to the aspect of the waterway.

The Vistula here, with its considerable rise and fall, according to the seasons, its banks of high, uncertain bluff, and its improvised buildings on the further edge of the stream, and its river steamboats, strangely chimed in my spirit (and the memory of it still so chimes) with the Ohio. This may sound grotesque, I know, but I am telling the truth as to what passed in my own mind and to the memory of what has taken root there.

Warsaw, henceforward, will mean very much more than all this to every European concerned with the future of Europe; but with all that it is not here my province to deal.

Poznan

Poznan, the German name for which is Posen, is that city out of all Poland where the profound contrast and antagonism between the Poles and the Germans is perhaps most strongly apparent. It is of all Polish towns the one in which the outward and material effect of the partition and of the Prussian domination over western Poland, over the "Outer Crescent of Polish Land," was most evident. One did not see this at once. One did not find this among the people only—such contrast and antagonism among the people were present everywhere under Prussian rule, but it struck the eye the moment of entering the city from the railway station. One felt it more in Torun. In Cracow there was hardly any of it because Cracow had been under the more sympathetic rule of Vienna; but in Poznan it was clear, and one saw it in two outward senses which were very marked. First the contrast between the new quarters, the wide streets, and the rest, which were thoroughly German in appearance, but next, and much more, between the huge and hideous sham castle which stood up in its enormity, *swearing* violently with the old town. That contrast was the most striking of all.

I was told that this monstrous erection was proposed and sponsored by the last Hohenzollern monarch himself, and I can well believe it, but I was given no particulars of it and I read none. I repeat only what was told me in talk when I visited the town, now many years ago. That stamp of an alien dominion seemed in its ineptitude and blatancy not only out of touch with Polish things, but almost equally out of harmony with the older German spirit which had so much better and deeper roots than ever Prussia could strike. The Prussian side of Poznan was almost as much opposed to the aspect of, say, Weimar, as to the old Polish town itself. It did at least what it set out to do; it impressed itself.

After all these years that big annoyance still returns to me more vividly than any other thing I saw in my journey westward back from Poland. It affected me much as a loud and harsh voice will be remembered when other more pleasing experiences of some call paid to a friend's house would be forgotten. If you have ever been astonished and annoyed by such a noise in a decent drawingroom you will know what I mean when I speak with so much repulsion of the so-called Castle of Poznan.

Not far off, and behind all that, one comes to something as Polish as Poland can show—the old market place and town hall in the centre of the town. Close by this you will visit, if you are wise, one of the best local collections of Polish engraving and drawing which I know. This was then quite a small collection, but so thoroughly national and the examples so well chosen that to go through it was like meeting a personality; like becoming acquainted with a character, and a very pleasant character at that. The old houses around the place and the whole spirit of it were pleasant with that tradition and special culture which have made Poland what it is, and will, I fancy, survive all accidents of the present and the future as it has survived the accidents of the past.

I read and retained the very divergent figures given me in

what seemed to be impartial descriptions of the *members* belonging to the two communities which here mix very ill. By one account just over one-tenth—my authority said eleven per cent—were German in Poznan and just under nine-tenths Polish. By the other account the mixture was half and half: fifty per cent Polish, fifty German. That is certainly a great exaggeration the other way, and if it be asked how such a huge discrepancy between the two estimates can be, it may be replied that there is always something of the sort where hostile races and cultures meet, and when the gathering of official statistics is in one side to the exclusion of the other.

But it would give a very false impression to represent the town as being but superficially Germanised. For a century and a half oppression, brutal and unashamed, has worked for the destruction or absorption of the old and original Poznan. The Prussian spirit is therefore stamped very deeply upon its outward features, and to some extent upon its soul as well. Doubtless there has been also very considerable intermixture of blood in the process, and one better acquainted with the town than I might well insist on that mixed blood and the zone of German or Germanised people coming, as is claimed, to half the population. This character was, of course, enhanced by the impression of German architecture in the newer parts of the place. It was also clear that much of the capital, and luxury too, for that matter, was German. I read that in the neighbourhood nearly the whole land was in the hands of German owners, but only the stronger did the rivalry between the two spirits appear.

It was one of the first acts of Berlin after the overrunning of Poland to proclaim the re-annexation of this province to the Reich, and I am sure that to the Germans of my own generation nothing could seem more natural. For though the proportion of the old Polish kingdom which was ultimately seized by Prussia at the end of the eighteenth century was not so large as the part that went to the Russians, it had been more developed during the later nineteenth century, and Poznan, lying as it did not far from the cultural and linguistic frontier and standing on the main railway line running eastward from Berlin (and that frontier is barely 100 miles away), seems to the passing traveller, at least, more thoroughly incorporated with the Reich than any Polish town; yet, as I saw it, Poznan was fully Polish in essence, and perhaps more strongly so from its experience of suffering under detested foreign tyranny.

It must be remembered that Poznan, like so much else in Poland, preserves very strongly those old memories of a long past by which the Polish spirit survives, and will survive. Religion is the ally of these enduring influences of the past, and another of their allies is the subtle influence of family tradition. When the blood is mixed, whether the bulk of physical inheritance be Prussian or Polish, it is the Polish air that is breathed and the Polish subtlety that pervades and gives savour.

The soil and its waters conspire to the same end; for Poznan is a city of the Warter River, the second great stream of Poland and the avenue of Poland's western life, just as the Vistula is the avenue of Poland's central life. Thus it is that Poznan, however much its masters and colonisers have striven to obliterate the ancient meaning of the place, is still a city of the Throne. The kings of Poland held their court here far into the later Middle Ages, and the royal claim, though the monarchy changed so greatly and fell at last to be elective (which was its ruin), is retained.

You may go past the centre of the older town to the bank of the river that nourished the growth of the city, and standing there make certain that the presiding genius of those waters will outlive so many and so tragic changes, including this last, the most shocking and perhaps the most ephemeral.

The West knows little of Poznan and its story. To us of the Occident it is but a name, and for nearly all of us a name not native: imposed from without. But history develops not on fixed, still less on direct lines. The course of political change is devious; it meanders as the river of Poznan meanders through its plains; and who shall say to what end, in a century or less, the stream of time will bear this place upon the Polish towns? Who that knows the recurrent resurrections of Poland will affirm that the tale of them is concluded?

Cracow

CRACOW IS ONE OF THOSE TOWNS WHICH SEEM TO THE traveller exceptional from the moment he first comes upon them. This is in part because it is the first Polish town of importance, the first completely Polish town he comes upon as he goes eastward and north of the mountains away from the confused industrial mass of Silesia. But it is more exceptional and individual from its buildings and outward appearance than for any other reason.

The first thing that strikes a man coming in there from the West is that feature which gave Cracow all its meaning from the beginning—the isolated Castle Hill, standing splendid about the young river at its foot.

I have heard it compared to the castle hill at Edinburgh, but it is of a different quality: not so rugged, not so led-up to: something more apart. But, like the hill at Edinburgh, it is the cause and root of the place. Like the hill at Edinburgh, it bears its ancient fortress, but here at Cracow the fortress and the palace were all one. Here the Kings of Poland were crowned. Hence the story of the nation rightly proceeds. One might almost say that Cracow is Poland, and that upon this rock the surging tides of invasion, passing and swirling, have left no mark.

It is not for nothing that the citadel has a sort of historical sanctity about it deeply rooted in the soul of the Polish people. It is an emblem, and much more a symbol, of that undying thing which we of the West know so little, and of which we are now to learn so much more. I could wish that someone with a sense of storm, some painter who understood the value of dark impending clouds and of the bright sky beyond, had made a picture of that Wawel hill with thunder behind it to the north and the sun full on the crag. It would serve for a perpetual reminder of what Poland is, has been, and will be. We must remember how, at the recitation of the Creed, the Polish nobles drew their swords. We must remember also how the Tartar from the East went galloping by, and we must remember how, when the country was prostrate and its body carved up by enemies, Cracow still enjoyed some memory of its past and some ghost of its independence. Cracow is all that; and its famous hill is the banner thereof.

The hill stands with the castle that it bears, upon the edge of the city. That city spreads beyond to the left of the river over the flat. Within the castle enclosure lie the shrines of which the greatest must always be the tomb of Kosciusko. Below, on the farther side from the river, lie the houses and churches of the town.

Of the churches by far the first is one which, if it stood here in the West, would be among the most famous of human things. It is the church which is dedicated to the Mother of God, in which it does not differ from I know not how many thousand others from Paris downwards. But the peculiar glory of this building (which is in the late Gothic) is unity and coloured light. You come out of the market place into this shrine (of no very great size) as you might come into the inside of such a jewel as no precious stone Nature has made can furnish. I know not whether it be the effulgence of colours beyond the colours of this world or the form of the frame-work in which those windows are set, but I know that the total impact upon the mind is like nothing else that I have seen in Europe, and perhaps like nothing else on earth.

There is also about this building a certain character the name for which is not easy to find: it may perhaps best be called "domesticity." It belongs to its people and is at home. It has not been weakened by any pomposity of approach. There is no destruction around it of more ancient things. It is not announced to the traveller with that sort of flourish which always savours of pretence. The great cathedrals of the West have been for the most part treated in such a fashion, and their link with their own past has thereby been weakened. They are like men and women of the former time introduced in the costume of their day to a modern audience and made awkward thereby. Not so the church of Cracow. It has been made and grown where it is and is the centre of its own world. The market people come into it by its side door as when they come into any house of a familiar friend without introduction, but of a friend who has been the friend also of their fathers and their fathers' fathers without break of any kind for generations.

There are many other things to be said about Cracow. The walls, notably the northern gate, are formidable memorials (and preservers) of greatness. Though not continuous, they strongly impress the mind, and more so perhaps from the contrast between their outline and the modern extension of the city without (for Cracow has become, not for its own good, a modern city in its modern extensions, and counts, I believe, all told, a quarter of a million souls). The men and women in the streets are wholly themselves, part of their own people, and I found that it was in Cracow I first felt that strong air of a separate populace: a people till then new to me. It was in

Cracow that the Renaissance produced at its dawn in the fourteenth century the original university of what was most eastern in the old united Christendom, and that university still stands to-day. It will continue. It will support the resistance to alien things.

But all these memorials of Cracow in my mind are as nothing to the thing which most occupies me as I write: the undying quality of this outpost, of Poland, whereof Cracow is but the kernel of the jewel, though a most worthy one.

Neither I nor any of you who read this can say whether the trial will be long or short. The future is as completely cut off from us as it was from the men who suffered the Asiatic torture long ago, as it was from those who triumphed in the resurrection of the people after the first invasion, as it was from those who took arms against partition, once and again, and were once and again defeated: as it was from Pilsudski when he rode out with his first band. The understanding of history does not lie in the noting of events as they pass, but in their interpretation. In Cracow that interpretation is an interpretation of continuance, of the falling of the flood, of reappearance.

Moscow Remembered

I SHOULD LIKE TO GO BACK TO MOSCOW. I DOUBT WHETHER I shall ever have the chance, or whether I could take that chance if it came, but the interest of such a visit would be very great, not on the political side (with which I am not here concerned) but in order to renew my impressions of a quarter of a century ago and see what changes there are in the outward look of things.

I saw Moscow in 1912. I went there in connection with a book I was writing on Napoleon's Russian campaign, and for that purpose I visited also the line of his advance, paying special attention to Smolensk and the battlefield of the Moscowa which is also called Borodino. Then on my way back I paid equal attention to the crossing-place of the Beresina, which may be taken as the end of the retreat. Of special interest was that bit of country just to the east thereof where Ney and the fragments of his command lost themselves in the night (it was there that took place that little incident most appealing to the imagination: the Marshal breaking the thin ice over a small stream that he might see which way the water flowed and thus judge his direction as he peered through the broken surface by the light of a hand lantern).

But to return to Moscow—as I wish I could.

What I always find of interest myself in anybody else's account of a first visit to an unknown place is the earliest thing that struck them in it: the thing which impressed their first memories. This is commonly something insignificant and hardly ever a show place. In my case it is a matter between the two—the walls of the Kremlin. These impressed me vividly at once by their smallness. I could have repeated the very words of Napoleon when *he* saw them first. He said, "What walls!" That is exactly how I felt. Moscow is a very famous city, and the walls of a city are the most sacred thing about it. The walls of a famous city, especially of a city famous in war, should be, and nearly always are, something imposing: the Aurelian wall, for instance—but travellers tell me that the walls of Peking are even more impressive than the walls of Rome. Of everything in Moscow the Kremlin is best known by name, so I had looked for walls majestic and imposing. Instead of that, I saw something which might have been the boundary of an Italian private garden. They are low, crenellated things which one might almost think had been put up for ornament rather than defence. Indeed, I have read that the architect of them was an Italian, but that reading was so long ago that my memory here may betray me.

The next thing that struck me as I walked about the city was the surface of the streets. Like a great many other things in Russia, they reminded me of America, especially of the towns of the Middle West, new in my youth. It would be interesting to see what the new régime has done to those rough Moscow streets.

Next I noticed the fine sweep of the river and the way in which it mirrors the slight lift of the Kremlin above it. Here my reminiscence is vague and the visual picture in my mind has faded. It has also, I think, been confused by the pictures I have seen before and since of that sweep of water, but I certainly retain an impression of something almost majestic, although there was no height to lend dignity to the scene.

Next I remember (and this very vividly) the splendour of the churches from within, especially one great church in the Kremlin itself, the name of which I did not ask and do not know to this day. For I must confess to this weakness in travel, that I like to come across everything as though it were a discovery and to furnish my mind with visual memories rather than literary.

The last and most impressive thing of all as I look back over these twenty-seven years is the immense size of Moscow. Whatever it may be by actual measurement, the sacred town gives an impression of vastness which I have never seen equalled anywhere else. I know not how this arises. It may be because one has approached it through what felt at the time like endless voids of slightly rolling land wherein repeated woods stand like very low islands edged by cliffs of short trees. It may be because, before one comes to Moscow, one has seen similar village after similar village for whole days of travel: always the same church with the blue onion dome, always the same spreadoutedness, always the same rough tracks radiating out across the empty land. It may be the lack of stature in Moscow, the absence of any one towering thing which does give so strong a feeling of extension sweeping away on every side. Or it may be the means of progression, which, in the days when I was there, were roomy two-horsed carriages all jingling with bells. Such driving might go on for an eternity, one thought, as it took you through the capital. You have a sense that you are not going from any one place to any other one place in Moscow, but trotting at large through a province which is all Moscow, or (by another metaphor) swimming at large through an element which is all Moscow and never seems to end.

Were I ever to return (which I shall not) I would follow exactly in my footsteps of that first and last experience of the place, but particularly should I be careful to come alone by the big *chaussée* from the west which at a particular point, topping a rise of land, shows you the city below. In my time this glimpse or vision was held in religious veneration. I was told that men went down on their knees as at the first sight of a Holy Place. It had something of the same effect on the native traveller as the first sight of Jerusalem from the Emmaus Road had on the Crusaders.

Does that sentiment still hold? I doubt it! Will it return? That no man can tell. I have heard men who should know talk very learnedly on both sides, and as I am myself ignorant on it I kept silent during those discussions which I have heard in London and in Paris and in Rome from those who had known the Russia of old days: exiles and travellers. Of Russia as it is today no one in print or by speech has given me any recognisable picture at all. It is true I am handicapped or advantaged by not knowing one word of the language. I have found myself in this situation elsewhere than in Russia. It may seem eccentric to confess that such isolation enhances the visual impression and strengthens the memory of it.

The Low Countries

YOU COULD NOT HAVE A BETTER EXAMPLE OF WHAT TIME
does with States than the meaning of the words "Holland"
and "Belgium." The greatest of Greek philosophers said
that infinite time was the maker of States: for "infinite"
read "greatly extended," or "indefinitely long." But as a
rhetorical expression it is sound enough, and the same truth
is expressed by the pedants who keep on telling us that the
constitutional state cannot be made but must grow: as
though we did not know that already, and as though both
deliberate and rational planning *and* growth were not necessary to constitutions.

Anyhow, it is time that produces States. But it not only
produces a State, it also modifies it continually and in time
destroys it. Who today would die for Babylon? To whom
is the King of Egypt a divine incarnation of the people and
of the River? So when you look at a fixed State of your
own time always remember two things about it. First, that
not so very long ago it was not. Next, that, after some
added generations of men, it will not be. To these two add
a third: that in coming to be what it is to-day, the State
has passed through a prolonged and manifold development.

So it is with Holland and Belgium, which for centuries
were not known as nations, nor knew themselves as such;
and only quite late in the long European story began to
take on so definite a form. Yet if they are in the news

today, as they are very much in the news, it is because men are immediately demanded to dedicate their lives to the life of those two modern entities.

Our fathers knew all that district as the Lowlands, the Netherlands, Les pays Bas. You may call them the combined deltas of the Meuse and the Rhine. For the Scheldt does not carry so much silt in its much lesser stream as to contribute much to the mass of marsh and island which build up the maritime flats between the Germanies and the North Sea. The whole place is the combined delta of those two main rivers and, of course, much the most of it is the creation of the Rhine.

Everything about it was indeterminate. Rome seems to have fixed a political boundary, with the Rhine, including its last narrow outlet to the North, as the convenient mark thereof. But in blood and in speech and presumably in all customs of dress and food and tribal worship the indefinite districts of Marsh and Island and Forest faded one into the other.

We have no records worth speaking of till after the conversion centuries after the central rule of the Empire had broken down in the West. Then, when all things were renewed in the great spring of the early Middle Ages, the Lowland towns begin. They also were the creation of the Rhine, for it was trade coming over the Alps and then downstream all the way to the North Sea that made the growing cities of the Lowlands into markets where everything was exchanged and all currencies could be found mingling. But each town became virtually a republic, and the little districts round them and the separate districts with no very large town to form a nucleus for them, each held by a loose tie to some feudal lord. At first in the drier south and up to the Scheldt it was the Count of Flanders, more or less responsible to the King in Paris. But to the east of him and to the north of him, the lesser feudal and urban divisions felt themselves rather to be under the Emperor.

There was no natural frontier, whether to the east or to the south. The thing that stands out for us is the division of dialects: local forms of speech akin to northern French in one belt and then beyond it forms akin to the Low German, or, rather counting with the Low German for century after century.

Quite at the end of the Middle Ages there came for the first time some sort of common link to these flats, which had by that time become a country of immensely wealthy cities. The House of Burgundy had patiently acquired by marriage and claim an overlordship which was in no sort of way a conquest but a natural political happening. To this day popular tradition looks back to the Burgundian rule in the Netherlands (that vague paternal authority which left the towns and provinces so free) as to a golden age. This is in part because the later Burgundian rule was thoroughly native, of double speech, with the Teutonic commonest but the Gallic—that is the Latin, the Northern French—more official and the idiom of the ruling House. But it was also and more because the Burgundian age was a moment of maximum wealth just before the social and political earthquake of the early and middle sixteenth century.

Accident put the right to govern the Netherlands into the hands of the Prince of Spain, a Habsburg. Further accident led to special taxation, hitherto unknown, and imposed upon merchant-princes and their citizens, who had hitherto felt themselves to be their own masters. The new enormous and intense religious quarrel did the rest. There followed on it a fierce anarchy, a fierce repression thereof, by what was the best soldiery in Europe—the Spanish; but alien indeed to the Netherlands. Then, after a confusion as violent as eruption and lava in the cone of a volcano, the Lowlands fell back to themselves, crystallised, as it were, into two divisions which were to be the beginning of two new States—the one which is to-day the kingdom of the Netherlands, the other which is to-day the kingdom of Belgium.

It was in the memory of the men we knew, men who had reached old age before the close of the nineteenth century, that the last attempt at uniting the Lowlands under one authority broke down. The southern half, which inherited from the united religious traditions of Brussels and of the southern Flemings, rebelled against the garrisons of the northern half. A new Royal House was set up to be a centre and symbol for the first; the same Royal House of Orange continued to be a centre and symbol of the second.

It is just over a hundred years, though not yet one hundred-and-ten, since that last settlement originated. Time has once more established or "made" two nations. But he is unquiet. He will be at it again.

Falaise

There are towns in Europe which are half or quarter famous and deserve much more fame, not for special beauty, though there is commonly something beautiful about them, but on account of their history. Among these I reckon Falaise, in Normandy.

So many people have seen it or passed through it, and so many English travellers have heard of it through its connection with William the Conqueror, that it has got a certain measure of recognition; happily not enough to have spoilt it in any way, but enough to make some of my readers wonder why I should devote a column to it as though it were something undiscovered. I cannot forbear to return in spirit to Falaise and write of it here, because at the middle of the summer of last year, if summer it could then be called, I returned to the town after many years. I was delighted to find it the same; if anything, a trifle more lonely than of old, and all the better for that. Anyhow, it was not travelling weather, even for hardy northerners, and under the persistent rain Falaise drooped and was silent, yet was still what I had known it to be for nearly fifty years.

Falaise has only one new thing in it, and that is quite a worthy one; it is a bronze statue of its most famous son, William the Bastard, caracoling on his horse and brandishing a battle-axe to great purpose. I remember no allusion to William's wielding a battle-axe at Hastings, and the horse, his mount, is not of the right kind. He was riding, if I remember right, when he went down Telscombe Hill and charged heavily up the other side, a Spanish horse, one therefore presumably with Arab blood, and a rocking horse tail. But anyhow his metal horse at Falaise is mettlesome enough and will serve. It reminds me of what the critic said about the old song: "I fear no foe in shining armour"; for the critic hearing it answered, interrupting the singer, "You would if you saw him coming at you." William of Falaise, as he prances so vigorously in his home-town to-day, would certainly give pause to anyone whom he might be approaching in anger, or even half in jest.

The room in which tradition says he was born, a small dark corner in the thick walls of the castle, can hardly have changed since the eleventh century, which had the honour to welcome him. From its window you look down the sheer cliff and drop of stonework to the stream below, where there is still, I am glad to say, a tannery at work, as there was when William's grandfather (who, I take it, rather gloried in his daughter's shame) also pursued the trade of a tanner more than 900 years ago. That tannery is as fine a piece of continuity as I know in Europe, though continuity may be enjoyed in many places (for instance, the original small church of St. Hilary of Poitiers). But I, for my part, feel continuity more when there is continuity of occupation, as well as of site; of man's labour as well as of material things. And I can remember no other spot where you can find this complete continuity so perfectly as at the tannery beside the stream and beneath the castle rock of Falaise.

Falaise is interesting also to the gunner, and whatever is of interest to the gunner is important, for gunners are notoriously the most intelligent of mankind. It is of interest to the gunner because it is one of the early examples of precision at what was, for the time, a fairly long range. During the Wars of Religion, just over four hundred years ago, the Huguenot artillery was set up in battery on the opposing cliff which faces the castle of Falaise, and I have read that its fire shook the defences. Now the effect of artillery upon the stone walls of the Middle Ages did not begin to be serious with the first mere advent of the gun. It began to be serious when you could be fairly certain of planting each big round stone shot in the close neighbourhood of the spot where your last shot had fallen. It was the repeated blows of the heavy missiles coming upon the same stones in succession that effected a breach. In the early days of artillery there was no sufficient precision. Castles could not stand permanently against heavy fire, even in the early sixteenth century or late fifteenth, but they could stand against a short bout of it until the delivery became more accurate about a lifetime on.

For centuries as you came into Falaise by the Paris road from the far side, the south-eastern side, the opposite end of the town to that on which the castle stands, you would have seen the huddled houses built all altogether in a nest beyond a ravine, much like that other ravine over which the castle towers; then to the north again was yet another valley, so that the whole place was defended by nature against attack, and I have no doubt that this was the origin of it, as of its name. Men settled there because it could not be rushed. There is but one approach without natural interruption, and that is by the road from the west, just under the castle walls. Everywhere else the burgesses of Falaise were safe from attack until gunners became what they were after the end of the Middle Ages.

A last thing to be said of the town is praise for its two

churches, in the very last of the Gothic, and the best of them, I think, though that is perhaps my own bad taste in being always strongly attracted to the extremes of loveliness, is the Church with the archway over the road, the westermost of the two. (I do not know its dedication.) I shall always maintain that the very last of the Gothic was the best in the way of beauty. I know that is heresy, but I glory in it, like many another better man. It would seem as though the very end of any development, like this very end of the pointed arch, of the dream of the Middle Ages, produced a climax of beauty.

It would seem as though beauty were the natural accompaniment to the last expression in the decadence of a great time. Not if it breaks down slowly or vulgarises, but if something is eating it from within, as did a sort of moral cancer eat out the heart of the Middle Ages at their close. And if you want to know how excellent the last of the Gothic can be, go and look in this country at a modern building, vividly inspired by it, I mean the University of Bristol. Why that triumph is not universally famous I can never understand—or, rather, yes I can.

The Castle Called "Gaillard"

IF I HAD MY WAY, EVERYONE WHO HAD BEEN TOLD ABOUT any place should be told its "why"; but no one ever has their way, so we need not linger on that.

People should always be told *why* this city which they visit rose where it did, *why* that road passes where it does, and *why* even this ruin of the past stands in such and such a place.

So with the castle called "Gaillard," which means "The gallant, the challenging castle."

It stands, or stood, as all the world knows, on a not very high projecting tongue of chalk upon the right bank of the Seine, some distance down stream from the point where that river leaves the disputed Vexin which was the borderland between the Dukes of Normandy and their feudal superiors—in name, their overlords, in practice, their equals —for centuries: the Kings of Paris.

It must have been splendid indeed, in its first and brief full fighting life, which lasted not more than seven years. Richard the First, the Crusader, built it on his return in 1196-97; it was lost in the general forfeiture of John, his brother, when the King of France, Philip Augustus, took it at the end of an interminable siege. From that moment, it lost its purpose. It became a habitation. It warred no more; and now it is only a great ruin which the crowds of modern travel pass when they come to the crossing of the river at Les Andelys or (if they have that good fortune) as they move up or down the stream below. But why was the castle there?

What does that ruin mean?

Why did the King of France make that very great winter effort so prolonged and so wearing, and why until it was successful, and the place was in his hands, could he not count on holding Normandy?

The reason was this: that Château Gaillard blocked the avenue of approach from and to Normandy for the Dukes and for the Kings, the rivals. Water carriage was the easiest, the cheapest, and the most rapid kind of transport. The Seine was the great waterway leading on from the Channel to Paris. Astraddle of the Seine, and holding the mouth of it, was the ancient Roman province, the Five Bishoprics, the original lands of the five tribes; which lands, after the Empire had given over their government to the hands of the Scandinavian Chief and his dependants, came to be called "Normandy."

All the sweep from the Breton border to the Picard, when it came under the one ruler from Caen and Rouen meant the lower basin of the tidal Seine, and therefore he who was Lord of Normandy held the communications of Paris. It was not only for revenue, nor for the increase of land and direct sovereignty that the Capetian swallowed up the inheritance of the Plantagenet; it was especially because Normandy was the original and chief part of that inheritance, the main province which held Paris in its grasp. The rest—Anjou and Maine, and Poitu—made up much more, but only Normandy held the gate.

Now towards the end of the tidal Seine, at the very limits of the tide, a castle holding a sufficient garrison would cut and command the river traffic. It was the business of a castle on that scale to receive (if they were in peril) and to protect permanently a sufficient number of armed men and their mounts, so that these should threaten the communications on either side of them for a long day's ride. An army advancing on Normandy, that is, on Rouen, an army advancing to clear the valley of the Seine, must first take Château Gaillard; for until that was taken, its communications, if it went further, would always be in peril. Therefore did Philip Augustus spend on the seizing of this one point, the energy of a campaign. There were very few points of more importance to the Crowns of France and England in the early Middle Ages. When Château Gaillard fell Normandy had fallen with it.

The great stone castles, the product of the Crusades (or perhaps of the Spanish reconquest and the generation just before the Crusades), dominated all military effort from well before 1100 until well after 1500. Their decay was more gradual than people think. They retained some value still, on into the seventeenth century, and when Richelieu began the systematic destruction of the great keeps, when Cromwell in England followed the same model, half a lifetime later, even then castles were not completely ended.

It was not gunpowder which destroyed the castle; gunpowder was in full use for generations before the castle gave up the game and yielded to earthwork. What destroyed the castle was the slowly achieved accuracy and reliability of siege artillery.

Until the heavy gun could deliver its missile fairly frequently and within a certain margin of error upon its target, stone walls could withstand its attack. Indeed, until very late, the battering ram was more effective than cannon. But once you could be sure that your heavy ordnance would deliver, reasonably accurately and reasonably rapidly, blow upon blow upon a limited surface of stone the wall was doomed. It took a long time for men to find that out; they began by buttressing the wall with earth; they went on to make banks of earth outside, for one could not batter down earth as one could batter down stone. But the change was slow, and men were not fully awake to it until the coming of modern armies. It is amusing to note that on the lists of Continental fortresses you sometimes come upon walled cities—for instance, Carcassonne—ranking as strongholds and charged to the national treasury even in the nineteenth century.

Whenever a man makes a map of a countryside of the Middle Ages, or the first century and a half after them, he would do well to plot on it all the castles, distinguishing between their various rates, from a first-class fortress like this of Château Gaillard, to the half-fortified houses which swarmed all over the West. Having done this, he should mark on this map the lines of communication which each castle threatened, closed, or held, he should note what garrison each castle would protect and the radius of its action.

Some day the thing will be done, but I do not think it has yet been done. There is plenty of detailed work on the growth and development of the individual castles, and even on castle building as a whole, but (to my knowledge, at least) there is not anything covering the strategic work of the castle over any one great area. It might be done for England first of all.

St Vaast

DURING THESE WEEKS WHEN THE FIERCEST WAR HAS BEEN
thundering through the Artois, the world has had more to
do than to consider the lost beauty of the past. But to some
(and I am one) the destruction of beauty ranks very high
in the scale of tragedies. We shall not know for a long time
to come, I suppose, that fate of St Vaast and its tower;
but if it has gone, or if it disappears in the subsequent
fighting, then there will happen one of those very rare
double murders of beauty which are the mark of our time.
I mean by "double murders" the destruction not only of the
original thing in a first war, but the destruction of its carefully built restoration in the course of a second war within
a quarter of a century.

I was in Arras, the capital of the Artois, twice or perhaps
three times when it was held by British troops during the
Great War and when the enemy lay almost immediately
outside. If I remember aright, the No Man's Land (of
which I have a photograph here at home where I am writing) began a little outside the railway station. Building
by building, as the war proceeded, Arras suffered a partial
ruin. That was the fate of all towns standing near or upon
the front.

But Arras had a monument of its own, so to speak; a
special example of ruin that could not be matched elsewhere. In the centre of the town near that very fine square

with its Flemish arcades, which also suffered so severely during the long months of conflict, there had stood for centuries the monastery of St Vaast. Vaast was the Flemish form of Vedastus. Vedastus lived in the time of the Great Conversion, when all the Roman Empire was changing from the pagan to the finally Christian form. It was he who prepared Clovis for baptism. He came up to this borderland of the Artois missionising. He made Arras his centre, and when he died he was buried there.

Seeing what a great part he had played in the transformation of Northern Gaul, his tradition grew enormously and the Benedictine abbey of Arras took on his name. St Vaast it became and St Vaast it remained for thirteen hundred years. Now the striking thing about that abbey was this: that during the Burgundian and Spanish rule over this part of the Low Countries a certain local type of architecture arose exactly consonant with the spirit of the people; a true reflection of their spirit, of that richness in detail bordering on extravagance which you find in all the cities of that wealthy land. There was raised high above the roofs of the monastery such a tower as I do not remember to have seen anywhere else in Europe: carven and recarven, piled with fantasy in stone, not exactly what we call Gothic, still less Spanish (though it had a Spanish aroma about it). It is no good trying to describe it, especially if you are a man who, like myself, is ignorant upon architectural things. The point about this tower of St Vaast was that it filled the memory of anyone who had seen it. At least, it certainly filled mine.

It was the most unfortunate fate of this glorious thing that after it had stood for so many generations (I suppose it must have dated from the early sixteenth century), it became the victim of modern guns. It was not wantonly destroyed, as was Louvain. It was destroyed by repeated blows because it formed so excellent a watch-tower; the enemy could not afford to leave it standing, so he battered it down, lest observation from it should continue; for the summit of St Vaast tower dominated all the Arras battle-field.

When I came back to the town after the Armistice and could note the extent of the destruction, everything paled before the murder of St Vaast tower. The glorious old Flemish houses in the greater and the lesser market-place, the eighteenth-century sober but well-decorated private houses (most of them untouched but some few collapsed), the details of carving here and there chipped off by splinters of a shell, the gaunt empty shell of the cathedral—none of these moved the spectator as did that high ruin of St Vaast tower, gaping against the sky. I remembered it as it had been when I had last seen it at the very end of the last century, intact and glorious. I certainly thought it could never be revived.

But the town and the State took on the task here as they did at Rheims, and with the same astonishing success. Gradually, stone by stone, an exact replica of the old tower reappeared in the Artois air and under the Artois sky. When I saw the thing completed I felt the same admiration and surprise as when I saw the rebuilt and restored campanile in Venice, which was and is another miracle of rebuilding.

But the campanile at Venice had a better fate. For it did not come under fire again in another war as Arras has now come.

When shall I know what has happened to Arras?

Not for months, perhaps. It may have been bruised or wounded or killed again after that first rising from the dead. And so it is all over the land where the insane vanity of barbarism destroys and destroys and destroys.

Avignon

AVIGNON HAS ALWAYS BEEN A CROSSWAYS AND A MEETING
place: an establishment in Europe. It became of the very
first importance more than six hundred years ago at the
turn of the fourteenth century. It has remained important
ever since, specially visited and specially known; so there
seems very little to say about it that can be new to anyone.

And yet I remember learning this, that and the other
about it all during my life of travel and almost every year
finding some unexpected thing.

For instance, I did not know for a long time that the
walls of this most famous of walled cities had been preserved by something like an accident. I hear that there was
a time (when progress was in full spate, perhaps a lifetime
ago, or perhaps a century), when it was proposed by the
people of the place to pull down the walls. Those walls
were old-fashioned and *that* was against them; but plenty
of other reasons could be found for supporting the policy.
The walls prevented people walking at will in and out of
the town. They prevented a natural expansion, and that was
hard lines on those who owned land just outside. They
were (then) half ruinous.

There are always any amount of arguments for or against
anything. But luckily it so happened that the proposal
came at a moment when the Romantics were strong and,
as you may imagine, medieval walls were sacred to the

Romantics. They uttered great cries and the walls of Avignon were saved. They were not only saved but restored, and there they are to this day to show the passer-by what walls of towns were in the later Middle Ages. Among other things they showed the problem of size. If you make your wall too high it is difficult to man it quickly from within, also it costs more and more (after a certain point) in geometrical proportion to its height. If you make your wall too low it can be the more easily scaled: the assault does not need such long ladders, and what is more can be attacked in more places at once. The walls of Avignon are low because the circuit was great, too great for the mercenary garrison of the Papal town. They were only just high enough to meet attack.

Another thing about Avignon is this: that it was the starting point of that great change in Europe when a highly centralised Court of Appeal and Treasury System gathered round the Papacy. The seeds of these were, of course, far earlier; but after the exile of the Papacy at Avignon those things took on a new importance and were an increasing peril to the institution which they served. So when you look on that very fine cubical mass of masonry, the Castle of the Popes, you are looking at one of those few places in Europe which were the home of an outward and inward revolution rather than of that more common thing a gradual development.

I know of no human work which more impresses the mind with a sensation of towering height than does this same Palace of the Popes overhanging the very deep, narrow lane which skirts the southern side of the building. What it is which thus produces the effect of height in any human thing, I have often sought but never discovered. Beauvais, from the inside, looks so high that it seems a creation beyond human power, but the Eiffel Tower does not look high. And so this unbroken wall above that Avignon alley, which is but a tenth of the height of the Eiffel Tower, tells you as you pass that it is the highest wall in the world.

Yet another thing about Avignon is the mark set upon it by the Black Death. That is a mark which has been set upon innumerable places in Christendom; Beauvais and here in England, the church of Great Yarmouth, and in the south, Narbonne.

In each case men began to make a thing on a certain scale and then were suddenly pulled up sharp by an awful, a complete, a universal disaster—and what they had begun was never finished. The mark of the Black Death at Avignon is, they say, the uncompleted bridge across the Rhone. It was a very difficult enterprise for the day in which it was undertaken. But the new Papal Court had come with its revenues drawn from all the west and swelling like a tide; in spite of the difficulties and the repeated breakdowns, the bridge would have stretched at last to the island and thence westward to the further bank, nor was anywhere a great bridge more needed than here on the lower Rhone. But after the Black Death men lost heart, repaired less, and now only the fragment remains.

Yet another thing about Avignon is (as with Arles, as with Vienne, as with all these towns on the racing, turbulent, everflooding, and devastating Rhone) the impress of unfathomable antiquity. The great rock (which, from the cathedral it bears, is called the Doms) was a refuge for men when first they began to gather in a tribal centre and to make the beginnings of towns. There have been found upon it the earliest weapons. There, we may believe, was also the first worship established in Avignon. To what gods? With what rites?

Standing on the platform of that height you can survey

the valley in one sweep as from nowhere else between Lyons and the sea, or at least as from no other urban vantage point. Thence also you may see that great wave-like lift of the Ventoux which is the guardian of everything around. They have today, I am told, a motor road up all those thousands of feet to the summit of the Ventoux. We may deplore or applaud the achievement. For my part I deplore it.

Standing there also on the platform of the rock of Avignon, right over the rushing stream, you may meet and understand the Mistral as you will meet and understand it nowhere else. The Mistral does not lurk or hide, it advertises itself most unmistakably—that piercing wind, cutting with cold like a sword and charging at an irresistible charge down the funnel of the Rhone Valley, is something which even the chance passer-by remembers all his life. As with height, so with cold and speed, it is not to be discovered what makes this special effect. There are winds colder than the Mistral to be met with over half the earth. There are gales of more volume, perhaps even fiercer and certainly moving at a greater rate. But there is no wind which can challenge the Mistral for its quality of deathly command. It comes to defy and cow the race of men wherever it strikes, and you know it at once, even far out at sea, for what it is.

And yet another thing about Avignon is that here did I come across the first American rocking-chair that ever met my eyes on this side of the Atlantic. I was young when I was greeted by this sudden stranger, but had already known the States from ocean to ocean. I said to myself, "They are coming."

La Rochelle

ONE OF THE MOST INTERESTING PLACES ONE COULD STILL get to easily during Peace, in spite of Progress, is La Rochelle. It is of special interest to Englishmen in a general fashion and in a particular. It is of general interest through its position in religious history, being perhaps the most famous of all the Huguenot towns and still holding a strong Huguenot tradition.

Montbeliard is another town in the same religious tradition and one that was equally open to travel without vexations, but Montbeliard had not the same long-rooted religious history as La Rochelle in connection with the struggle in France; for it was not part of French territory till long after the religious wars were over. La Rochelle, on the contrary, is of the very heart of those religious wars; and to the general traveller will recall little else; but La Rochelle has, as I say, particular interest for Englishmen because it was the object of Buckingham's expedition in the first years of Charles the First's reign—the adventure which by its expense and failure led up to the King's main quarrel with his parliament.

La Rochelle was under siege in Charles the First's reign. The forces of the French Crown had sat down before it to reduce its local religious privileges. On the success or failure of that attempt would depend all the future of Richelieu.

Charles fitted out an expeditionary force to succour the
seaport and if possible raise the siege. It was a fine little
armada, one might almost call it a big one; it transported
English troops to the island of Ré, which lies off the harbour of La Rochelle. All, or nearly all those troops, were
English, and the whole business is an integral part of
English national history, not concerned with that foreign recruitment or alliance which often cuts across the
English military story.

Buckingham landed his troops on the Ile de Ré, and
very nearly succeeded in permanently occupying it. He
failed because the only fortified town on the island, St.
Martin, was sent provisions from the French mainland in
a successful raid which was a ten to one chance. Buckingham withdrew his men fairly successfully; he showed
the utmost courage throughout and conspicuous military
talent as well; but because he lost and because he was, in
England, on the royal side which later history made unpopular, neither his energy nor his talents have been done
justice to. (If you don't like a sentence ending in a prep-
osition, I do. It is the very genius of English.)

Later, after Buckingham had been murdered another
expedition went off under his brother-in-law, Denbigh;
but by that time the conditions had changed and the relief
of La Rochelle was no longer possible. Had Buckingham
succeeded, the island could have been held by England
with her superior sea-power and it is probable that La
Rochelle would not have had to submit: in which case it is
not inconceivable (though less probable) that religious history in France would have been modified.

In a little square of the town, opposite the fine old
town hall, is a statue of the stocky little fellow who defended the place, and was mayor; a champion at once of
the Huguenot cause and of the town. He has a fine swag-

gering carriage, consonant to all that we read of him, a determined fellow; a diehard of the deepest dye. He bellowed defiance—if the word "bellow" is not too undignified a one to use of so brave a man.

Though the old town is not very large, you can spend a day and more wandering about it, because it is so full of things. There is not only that old sixteenth-century town-hall which I spoke of, but a mass of old houses and arcades, and, on every side, the atmosphere of the seventeenth century, of the days in which La Rochelle was most famous.

Being what it was for centuries, and on a small scale, and still is, maritime, the port of La Rochelle is what you will perhaps remember best about the place. I know not whether you will be struck, as I was, by its small size measured by modern standards. The thing one perpetually notices in the old havens is their smallness. It is one of the marks in which Europe has most changed; for there has been greater expansion in the tonnage of vessels and in their draught than in any other matter since antiquity—save in the area of that much less pleasant and much less interesting thing the industrial town. When one looks at these little ports (like so many here at home, Boston for instance or King's Lynn or Lyme Regis) one is astonished to think what great matters started from them. Honfleur is the same and I know not how many others all round the coast of the Continent. Most of them have been enlarged, but the old port of La Rochelle is happily unchanged.

It nearly dries out and is a mass of mud at low water; another common feature of these ancient things and one that makes me muse upon a certain problem. Since the little ports have been silting up from the beginning of recorded history, how comes it they are not by this time all dry land?

The port is famous also for the two towers which guard

the mouth of it. They are nearly 600 years old, and they look it. They were built both to fire from against enemies and to support the chain which was stretched across the mouth of the harbour to block it during hostilities; and that is why the western one is still called "the Chain Tower."

This little old port stands at the head of a long narrow bay, which helped to break the run of the sea and so gave further security to the haven. It was across this bay that Richelieu caused to be built the mole, which cut off La Rochelle from succour during the siege and from provisioning. They thought it a prodigious work at the time, and the trace and remains of it are still impressive. It still has a sort of material symbolism about it (though you can see very little), if only for the length which it had to straddle from shore to shore. Richelieu was familiar with the place as a younger man. The little town of Luçon, of which he had the bishopric as a sort of family living, is only a few miles to the north; and the family estate was all in the same country.

Now La Rochelle has been preserved for our benefit by the building of a new big modern harbour, La Pallice, a few miles off on the main seacoast. It is the terminus for transatlantic traffic as well as an important base for submarines. The making of this new big port, which reminds one of the same sort of thing all over Europe (Penzance and Newlyn, for instance, or Weymouth and Portland), has fossilised La Rochelle, and we cannot be too grateful for such preservation.

The Ardennes

ARISTOTLE, OR SOMEBODY ELSE, SAID THAT A THING ONLY WAS what it was in relation to other things. That is true. For instance, a cat is one thing to a mouse and quite another thing to you and me; and one's direction towards one star is up in New Zealand and down in England. I find today that for the second time in my life this applies to a bit of country I know very well, the Ardennes Forest. I had never thought when first I knew it, walking about therein as a young man, that it would mean what it meant in 1914, and again what it means today. I never thought I should think of it in terms of a war upon the Gallic and German Marches. Yet, after all, that is what the Ardennes have meant almost from the beginning; and I might have guessed that they would come to play their old part again in a new time.

What the Ardennes have done throughout history is to deflect Gallic military movements on their way to the Germanies, and German military movements on their way to the Gauls, to the right and the left of the obstacle which the great forest forms. It is due to the Ardennes that the lines of advance either way have lain between those woods and the North Sea or south of them by the Moselle Valley and through Lorraine. But there is one exception to this, and a most interesting one: the trench of the Meuse, where it runs through the Ardennes country. The great river pierces not only the woodland belt but the high hills in its centre after a fashion which rivers have and which (if the geologists will forgive me for saying it) no one has ever explained. The passage is one of those tortuous clefts which great streams follow, sometimes, through hills without our being able to conclude what dug them. Sometimes we know that they are trenches slowly dug out by a receding waterfall. But in most cases there is no evidence of that at all. The steep and profound valley swings from side to side as though it had been made by erosion in some great rush of water; but there is nothing to show why that rush of water should have taken place and no proof that it worked by erosion either.

Anyhow, such a valley, on the model of many another gorge in Europe, distinguishes the passage of the Meuse through the central Ardennes, and very fine it is. I have often wondered how the lining of the frontier with troops was arranged up that gorge, by Givet. The troops guarding a frontier could hardly hold so sharp a V salient. The salient of Givet was thus thrust into Belgium through an arrangement made at the end of the wars of Louis the Fourteenth. I seem to remember that this arrangement was made in order that the French Crown might keep a fortified point corresponding to the great stronghold of Namur at the other end of the defile. But, whatever the reason, the salient of Givet still stands there most strikingly: an anomaly on the modern map as it has been on all maps for now much more than two hundred years. Along the river through that gorge runs a good road and a main railway, and the river itself bears traffic; so the passage is important, but to right and left of it stands the great obstacle of the Ardennes.

It is not a continuous growth; it is a forest in the old

sense of the word; that is, a bit of "outland"; something which was not included in the manorial system, because it was not fertile and was ill-populated. But the Ardennes, as a whole, is full of great open spaces, heaths and clearings; its woods may once have formed one uninterrupted sheet hiding the Gallic land from the Germanic; but now they are no such thing.

As you travel through the Ardennes you have trees as your companions everywhere; but not everywhere in dense ranks. Where you find them thickest is upon the sides of this same gorge and again in the river valleys of Luxembourg. The Ardennes are no longer a continent of woodland, as it were; but an archipelago of woodlands. Nonetheless, if, when peace returns, you will take a month's leisure walking about therein you will come back with a memory of woodland everywhere; and you will understand why all the people of the Ardennes think of themselves as hunters and foresters, even to this day.

In that connection, notice the inn signs and remark how many of them are taken from the wild boar and the deer. Would that I had space to give you a list of those guest-houses, for I have known many of them; but the one that was the best of all has disappeared through the effect of the last Great War. Its disappearance was a very good example of how wars may do harm in unexpected ways. It was not burnt down nor ruined by shell. It was even used as a comfortable Headquarters, at one moment, by an enemy Army Corps. And when I visited it once more with all the joy of finding a recovered friend after the Armistice in '19 it was what it had been for generations; and even its splendid great cellar was still well-stocked.

What killed it then? Gold. Not lead, not iron, not fire, not guncotton; just gold . . . but when I say gold, I mean, of course, being a modern man, paper.

The thing came about thus: The world having taken pity on a ruined people, great sums were given to those who had suffered invasion. Among these was a family owning the famous inn. What did they do with the unexpected windfall? I will tell you. They pulled their patrimony down; the one thing by which they should have been glorious. They destroyed those fine old rooms and those majestic windows. And they put up in place of what had once been there a neo-Gothic horror after the fashion of a railway station hotel. Full of every convenience and luxury which make a house uninhabitable. When I came upon it it was worse than coming on something murdered; it was like coming upon a vile usurper in some palace of ancient lineage.

It was there, surrounded by the Ardennes, that, in the old days of peace, I had mused upon the story of those woods and had wondered upon their future which, happily for me, I did not know: for in those times the worse times into which we have survived were not yet dreamt of. I remember musing upon the name "Ardennes" and seeing that it must be the same as our word "Arden"; and I remember, after all these years, how pleased I was to look forward to looking up all the nonsense that pedants would have written upon the beginnings of a word on which they can know nothing, because it goes back right beyond history into the roots of things.

Luxembourg

THERE ARE TOWNS THAT SEEM DESTINED TO ENTER INTO ALL great modern European conflicts and yet get singularly omitted by fate. They will be mentioned in the course of a great war, but they seem under a spell which enables them to escape a peril apparently inevitable to them from their position. Aosta, Bale, Bellinzona are such—but especially is Luxembourg a town of this kind. It stands right in the path of armies and of a river-road in those border lands of the French and the Germans that are constant battlefields, yet it has been unhurt for generations—since long before living memory.

A lifetime ago in the Franco-Prussian quarrel before 1870 it looked as though the town and the independent little State of which it is the capital would inevitably be dragged in. It was not so. In those days there was still public law in Europe, and neutrality was respected.

During what we still hesitatingly call the "Great War" the neutrality of Luxembourg was violated by the march of the German armies, much at the same time those armies also invaded Belgium territory close at hand; but, luckily for all of us, there was no fighting on that neutral territory of Luxembourg. It was spared.

When I went back to it after the Armistice I found everything intact, and the people, though they had, of course, suffered from the conditions imposed by the blockade (as had indeed much of Northern France), were not burdened with any memories of active fighting. There was a comparatively small French garrison in occupation—one battalion, if I remember right; for the rest, great calm. I was glad to see things so, for I have known this happy little free district intimately all my life, one of the leading families in the place being close friends of my own people. Now it is again in some peril of interference from beyond its frontiers. I ardently hope it may be spared once more, for there is about these small independent countries in Europe a particular charm. They escape the burdens and the hatreds and the sufferings of the large States. They maintain a tradition of their own and a personal life of their own which is very attractive.

Luxembourg is German in texture. The popular speech is German, and it has become even more German, I think, in the last generation than it was when I first knew it as a boy. The wealthier classes speak French, or did all speak it as a rule until quite lately, but they are bilingual. There is no trace of intrusion such as elsewhere followed the establishment of the Second Reich close at hand. The affinity of the place was with Trèves, which, in spite of its having now been merged for so long into the much larger neighbouring State, kept until the eve of the Great War something of that same spirit of isolation and provincial character. For Trèves was, and, I hope, still is, one of the most pleasant towns in Europe.

But Luxembourg, unlike Trèves, was primarily a fortress. Nature had designed it for that part. Its original castle, the seed from which the town grew, stood on a high isolated ridge with profound and precipitous depth all around it. The men of the sixteenth and seventeenth centuries called it "The strongest place in Europe." Therefore, it has followed the changing fortunes of the border countries between the French and the German cultures. It counted as part of the Spanish Netherlands when the Crown of Spain came into the Burgundian heritage, and its architecture shows strongly in places the influence of the old Spanish occupation. You see this notably in the little pointed turrets overhanging the deep gorge which is the mark of the town and gave it so much defensive strength.

I can remember the days when this natural defence was still inviolate. Later, a great bridge was thrown in one very bold span from cliff to cliff, and today the main street from the station into the heart of the town goes over that surprisingly vast and not ungraceful arch.

The gorge which is the special characteristic of that landscape did not cut off the old town as thoroughly as such natural formations have cut off other similar places. Constantine in North Africa, for instance (which has much the same natural formation) is almost entirely cut off by its gorge, leaving only one narrow neck of land to connect it with the neighbouring plateau, while Luxembourg is joined on to its plateau by a broad approach of open land.

Luxembourg has long ceased to be a stronghold physically and has no such value under modern conditions: but morally it is a stronghold indeed. It is morally a stronghold because it is inhabited by strong local patriotism based on a healthy and vivid local and family tradition, and so maintains in the miserable confusion of the modern world one of the best things Christendom ever produced: a small independent State.

There was a time when men of German blood were apt beyond all other Europeans at producing and maintaining these happy little polities which could do no harm to any neighbour, which enjoyed their own personal life to the full, and by their diversity, by their humour, by their sense of the past greatly enriched Europe. Unhappily fashion changed. It became the fashion to worship what was called "power"—though it was not "power" at all, it was mere numbers: for there is no real power among men, save the power to create wherein man was made in image of God. These big overgrown, bullying modern States were not the product of long time (the only true maker of States) but are all rapid imitations. They breed nothing but evil continually. It was a very bad day for the Germans when they were tempted to follow this novel fashion to which they are unsuited and in which they are trapped.

But these small old German States of which here is one happily surviving, were perfect models of what a Christian Society should be. I should like to take Luxembourg for a criterion. I should like to come back some generations hence (this is improbable) and, finding Luxembourg still on its feet, say to myself, "All good things come to an end; but good things also survive." Which reminds me of the famous epigram, "Nothing leads anywhere, yet everything happens."

The Marble Rhine

I HAVE OFTEN CONSIDERED IN MY OWN MIND THE MINDS OF Inanimate Things. It is a futile occupation to which none the less I shall return, for habits grown firm and fixed with age. The Inanimate Things have, by definition, no emotions. It is no good worrying over what they think, for they don't think. Such attention to them resembles what goes on in the mind of a public man when he is consulted about public policy. His interlocutors—those who watch him—hang upon every muscle of his features and wonder in agony whether he is deciding for Monomotapa or Ruritania, whereas, as a fact, his mind is otherwise engaged, for he is wondering whether a stock called Paramookas will really go to five before settling-day, as a colleague confidently assured him.

Yet a contemplation of the Inanimate is a pleasant form of illusion, and I am willing to believe that the Higher Powers put us into some communion with the universe when we indulge in this innocuous pastime. The Higher Powers (henceforward to be called H.P.) say to themselves perhaps, "Poor beast! He is so limited by mortality that he is tortured with loneliness! Let us make him One with the Scheme of Things!" Whereupon the privileged meditonationist (if I may coin a term) pursues his meditations with profit to himself, though certainly with none to anybody else—but that doesn't matter: he does no harm.

Thus I had occasion the other day to study a large field
map of the Rhine in many sheets; I was even at the pains
of measuring ranges; but as I did so my mind wandered
off to a still more futile occupation, for I began to think
of the Rhine as an old marble gentleman lying propped
on one elbow and carrying under his other arm an urn
from which water flowed copiously. He also had round
about him reeds and weeds and even the adumbration of
little fishes. So had I seen him in a statue years ago. I must
apologise to my readers and admit that it was not a German
statue, though it does seem very wrong, does it not, for
anyone but a German to have made a semi-recumbent
statue of the Rhine as a divinity in stone? What right had
he to meddle with such a god if he were one of the in-
ferior races, Greeks or Italians or, more impossible still,
French?

But no matter; thus did there arise in my mind the image
of the Rhine, and I began thinking to myself how many
things the Old Boy had seen and wondering what he
thought of it all now.

They have never let him alone—which is a shame. They
are perpetually running over him like so many rats, back
and forth, pursuing their own ends, and leaving him no
peace. Yet, if I may trust the majestic though rather stupid
features of the image, nothing would have suited him better
than repose. He was made for majesty (by the sculptor,
at least, if not by his Creator), and in his simulacrum he
had a sort of paternal appearance mixed with a kind of
third-rate royalty. Also he was big—there was a lot of him;
and altogether he was satisfactory.

I should like to have seen a cluster of grapes added to the
monument, symbolising those vineyards which are the
Rhine's chief glory. I could do without the castles. Ruined,

they are theatrical; modern, they are appalling. But the
vineyards of the Rhine, though some think them of the
second class, are at any rate enduring and have their roots
in antiquity. It is not their fault that they came up from
the south, where the lesser breeds invented the uses of the
vineyard. The vineyards of the Rhine struck root so long
ago, and they have lasted so well, that there is a certain
nobility about them.

Next, I pondered within myself what old father Rhine
thought about mere words; mere sounds; mere language in
which he had been addressed. I should like to have ques-
tioned him on this point. What titles were given and what
prayers addressed to his difficult current in flood three
thousand years ago? Pedants have said that the men on the
Rhine banks talked a language which the pedants (and
nobody else) called "Celtic" long before any record was
made. Other pedants will have it that they spoke a language
called "Teutonic," which again means very little. It is a
comfort to remember that pedants are as ignorant of the
whole affair as we are.

One gentleman (if I may so call him) is delighted to
think that they talked Celtic on the left bank and even all
up the Moselle, because if that were true it would show that
people like himself who talk a Teutonic tongue came over
in invincible fashion as conquerors in the days before anybody bothered about these things. Another honest fellow
clings firmly to the imagination that they talked Teu-
tonically, because that would show that they had already
overflowed on to the western bank and thereby proved
their prowess. Yet another more acute and poignant man
will rejoice in saying that they were Celtic, because that
proves his right to come back again and worry the existing
inhabitants as did the King of France three hundred years

ago when he burnt the towns of the Rhine, using, by the way, for that purpose soldiers many of whom happened to be German. His brother will boast of ancestors on the left bank who were of his own kind and call them "Celtic" in order to prove that those ancestors were long ago very big people indeed. It is all criss-cross and contradiction.

Till lately the world was indifferent to the whole affair of "race," and, believe me, it will be indifferent again soon. The world will once more wrangle furiously, burn once more and massacre once more and otherwise disport itself as might be expected of mankind, but our descendants will find different occasions for their murderous activities; different excuses and different battle-cries from ours.

One thing I do wish, which is, that I could come back to this world and see what had happened to the Rhine two or three lifetimes hence. I have always thought mortality unjust. It has always seemed to me that we have a sort of right to continue, but, though I have had no personal proof of it, I am convinced that the thing cannot be done. Die we must. I know very well that I shall not stand again on the Colmar road in A.D. 2080 and look up at old Brisach on its rock as I did in happier days; nor know what new passions are making new troubles for the poor old river in between. But no matter.

The Alban Lake

THERE ARE CERTAIN PLACES THAT SEEM TO HAVE A SPELL OF endurance cast over them by protecting powers so that they do not suffer from the degradation of our day, or at least do not suffer from them so much as to break the heart of those who knew them in better times. In England Rye is one of these. In Italy there are many such islands of contented beauty and calm, and one that most often returns to my memory is the Alban Lake.

I was writing of it before the war in connection with volcanoes, for this famous but blessed and secluded piece of water is an old crater. It lies rather more than 1,000 ft. above the sea, some seventeen miles to the south of Rome, caught in a cup upon the slope of the Alban Hills and having immediately above it the palace or villa of Castel Gandolfo and the little town attached thereto. Around these detached and silent waters rise the steep slopes of a containing ring of hillsides, a ring closed everywhere without issue. Those ramparts are in part wood, in part pasture land, nowhere troubled by a road save on the extreme eastern edge, where (happily out of sight from most of the lake's neighbourhood) runs one of those great new ways of which the Italians are justly proud and which has here been designed very discreetly so that it opens up all that district of the Castelli without intruding upon it.

There are upon the eastern slope one or two houses

which have been built for retirement, notably the country house of the English College, and on the opposite shore are the few terraces and the houses attached to the main street of the little town and one or two of its inns. For the rest there is nothing but silence and the past. That past is so profound that one looks down into it for century upon century like a well.

Along the eastern shores of the water stood the mother town of Rome, Alba Longa, which has disappeared. I know not whether any relic of it remains. For it is a singular thing to be discovered everywhere in travel that towns are capable of complete disappearance, however famous, however long-lived, however strongly founded and built. There is one such disappearance most remarkable—that of Hippo Regius, the town of which St. Augustine was bishop in North Africa, in the ecclesiastical province of Carthage. It was a very great city; a considerable army of mercenaries, mainly Slav troops recruited from the Vandals, besieged it in 530 when St. Augustine himself was dying within its walls. What its circuit may have been I know not, but here and there a remaining fragment of stone, of broken wall, of discoverable pavement, indicates its area. It was very great and it has utterly gone. I have often asked myself how such a fate can overtake great masses of brick and squared stone, but certainly it happens. The place where the city once stood is as though that city had never been.

Alba Longa was, of course, nothing like Hippo Regius in size, but it had fame. It was the centre of the hill tribes. It was revered for its vast antiquity. And now there is nothing left.

The Alban Lake, like all those volcanic isolated water circles, has the quality of unexpectedness. The traveller who has not read up its neighbourhood, but to whom the approach is new, discovers it as a surprise. The same is true of the much larger Bolsena and of that astonishing little pond of Venus on the very apex of the high hill above Viterbo and of the larger Lake of Bracciano, in which is mirrored the only castle I know in Italy which might have got there from the North, so exactly does it reproduce all the features of our own and the French medieval strongholds. I have read somewhere that it was the thing in Italy which moved Sir Walter Scott more than all else, and I can well believe it for it is just like his novels.

When you come in by the main road to Castel Gandolfo and walk down the single longish street of the little town you could not guess that the lake was there until at one point, down by the end of the slight slope, you suddenly get a glimpse between the walls of an alley. You see the land falling away as from an overhanging terrace, and the lake lies far below you. I wonder whether this character of hiding away lent anything of mystery to those volcanic lakes and made them the religious things they were in the far origins of our story. The lake next to the Alban, the much smaller crater which has from the town on its banks the name of Nemi, had about it the most awful mystery of all. It was in the wood above its banks that the fugitive slave was lord for a brief while, having gained his title by the murder of the last one there, and himself to be succeeded by the newcomer who should murder him. "The slayer who shall himself be slain." I have heard of no such origins hanging round the Alban water, but the presence of it is enough to impress the mind permanently with things not wholly of this world.

When after the noise of Rome I used to withdraw to find peace and isolation, I, just before the war, found it on those shores. May they never grow famous! Perhaps some of those who read this will know that excellent hostelry which has housed me only this spring, and will house me again, I hope, in the future, for it is a refuge and a delight. Let anyone who knows it keep its name, if not secret, at least discreetly muted, for it hangs by a hair whether those shelves above the Alban water be ruined by modern transport or no. Hitherto they have been preserved, as such great places are preserved—we know not how. Perhaps they will be preserved indefinitely. So be it. But will it be so? Another memory makes me doubt it.

There was another such secret round of water nearer home, here in the North; a sea lake which, climate for climate, and soil for soil, might match the lake of Alba Longa. Yes! I have known it well! I remember in youth its austere majestic loneliness. A space of nearly fifty years divides me from the day when I first sailed into that separate peculiar haven, coming in all by myself under a small lug sail through the narrows which lead in from the outer sea. When the narrows were passed and the sheltered circle entered, even the sound of the outer sea was hushed, if not in fact, then in mind, for that place was made from the beginning for recollection and for peace. I lingered there in that hour of my youth enchanted, thinking I had found (as indeed I had) a jewel of this world—and hardly of this world.

Well, I came back to it after all that lifetime during which it had stood in my mind a changeless picture of calm and holiness. I came on it this time from the landward side, and long before I reached it the air was full of noise, and when I came to its shores they were crowded with hundreds or perhaps thousands: a soaring of voices, a clatter of engines and cries and exclamations and all that goes with crowds brought in to enjoy beauty in the modern fashion and to worship with modern clamour the goddess whose lips are sealed. It was as though all the strident and blind folly of our towns had been poured out upon this one innocent place for its damnation.

Yes! That can fall in so brief an interval upon an English paradise. Then who shall guarantee the Alban thing? Yet here I am, I myself, advertising it.

St. Peter's: Rome

WHEN I WAS PRESENT AT THE CORONATION OF POPE PIUS XII, I understood fully (and, I am afraid, for the first time) the splendour and satisfaction of St. Peter's.

It seems to be the only architectural work of Man which has exactly fulfilled its object. It was designed to be the Central Temple of the Catholic Church: that is, to be the home and roof and gathering place of a Society, universal, throughout the millions of mankind. Such a creation in stone must be a covering, a receptacle for man in the mass. It must receive, as its natural furniture, such myriads that the crowd of them shall be a symbol of the Church itself —and this with plenitude and without strain. It must have about it the note of complete success, although it deals with a spiritual and social fact beyond the power of human measurement.

All this, St. Peter's has achieved.

We have in the English language two words which, like so many words in that language, seem to indicate the same thing, but really stand for things very different. These two words are "bigness" and "greatness." It was above all essential to those who designed St. Peter's that they should achieve greatness. Mere bigness can always be achieved, without creative power and without vision. You have but to consider something already existing and multiply it by two or by ten or by a hundred; and that is the fashion in which the thoroughly imperfect and second-rate attempts to represent the sublime. Such a fashion invariably fails. In order to be great, a work of Man must be consonant to the nature of Man physical as well as Man spiritual. Make a thing too big for its function, and you had much better not have made it at all. There are buildings of far greater height, there are some no doubt of far greater content than this supreme triumph. But an increased height for that vast vault would have made it no longer a vault, but rather a mountain. An increase in bulk might have made it striking in a landscape, but would have dissolved its proportions as a building. It has been said that it dwarfs the human beings which gather before its altar. It does not do so when these are drawn together in the great crowds for which the shrine was intended. It emphasises the numbers, but leaves them human.

What is true of the scale of the thing is true also of its ornament. The ubiquitous gilding, the immense statuary, are consonant to the unity and personality of St. Peter's. Those who have sought and received violent emotion, those who have been trained in the romantic tradition which coloured the nineteenth century, do not appreciate what an inheritance they have in St. Peter's, for St. Peter's is the very opposite of the Romantic. It is the fullest type of the Classic—that is, of the artistic effort which does not attempt to say more than it can but is content to say even less than it might, and remains always within bounds.

It was in this case particularly difficult to work thus, because magnitude was of the essence of the thing to be done. The temptation to exaggerate was present always but, save in one matter (the length of the nave) was always resisted. Nor would the nave have been too long, I believe, had the original intention of Michelangelo been kept. For I have read that he intended the new St. Peter's of the

Renaissance to be on the plan of the Greek Cross and that its present form of a Latin Cross would not have fitted in with what he desired the whole, and especially the Dome, to represent.

For that is another matter in connection with St. Peter's which must never be forgotten: it is the creation of one mind, as everything that is to be supreme in its own department must be. No one could conceive of a great poem written by many hands—at least, no one has yet imagined such a thing excepting dons who think that the Iliad of Homer was written by a committee or made up of a patchwork. Unity—unity reflective of the unity of man's creative mind—is necessary to an enduring monument, and particularly if it be in the highest social tradition, which is the Classic.

Michelangelo himself was a man who at once gloried in and doubted his own complete fruition. His famous epitaph has in it more disappointment than glory. But I think that if he could survey his handiwork today he would be satisfied; though perhaps even such things as St. Peter's seem but toys in the *terra viventium*, in the *Patria* of the human soul. If this be not so, if what has been very well done by one man here on earth, a great building or a great poem or a great picture, deserves some recognition in Eternity, then certainly St. Peter's will take its place with the greatest of our Christian verse (or pagan, for that matter).

Moods have changed so rapidly in modern times, particularly since the turn of the Middle Ages in the fourteenth century, that it needs great strength of conviction to affirm permanence of any model. Things which appear to be the height of human power in one generation are ridiculed in the next. But I think that if we give the process time enough, full classical result will always come into its own and attain (so far as is possible for anything of mortal make to attain it) permanence. It has proved so with the summit of Greek effort and I believe will prove so with the summit of our Western effort, which I find here on that slight rise of ground overlooking Rome. This judgment on St. Peter's is not, at the moment, popular; a generation ago it would even have seemed ridiculous. Yet I confess to the conviction; I confess my adherence to it. It is more than an opinion. It is a conviction.

How many years has it not taken me to reach that point! I first came in under those timeless arches well over forty years ago. Only today do I see what they are.

Prague

IT IS A YEAR AND MORE SINCE ALL EUROPE BEGAN DISCUSSING Prague. The name has become a title, as it were, to the chief international problem of our times. As in the case of Danzig, the externals of the place are highly worthy of remark and memory, apart from the spiritual and racial conflict for which that capital stands.

Prague is one of those European cities which have been specially praised for their beauty, and the praise is just. But it seemed to me as I wandered through it a few years before the recent conflict that one might praise it even more for its individuality than for its beauty. It is a most *personal* town. I am not sure that you could say, were you to wake up of a morning in Prague and see it for the first time, "This is Slavonic. This is a fruit of the Slav mind." But I am quite sure one would say to oneself, if one saw Prague first suddenly, after having last contemplated a German city, "This is certainly not German." And yet the ruling power in Prague had been German ever since the Battle of the White Mountain, when the Hapsburg Emperor from Vienna, the Austrian, confirmed his legal right to the Kingdom of Bohemia. It was to affirm this right that he drove out his opponent, whom the Bohemian Nobles had chosen against him. This rival was that Elector Palatine who had wed the sister of Charles First, the English King.

The most striking thing about Prague to the eye is the

Castle, or Palace, standing beyond and above the river and overhanging the lower town. It counts in my memories with half a dozen human achievements in the way of building that triumph through their height: not so much height by actual measurement as the impression of height which they give. This sensation of height is imposed with something like violence, the main reason being, I suppose, the immense unbroken sheer blank wall plunging down from the fortress hill and its cathedral. It reminded me of pictures I had seen of the great palace at Lhasa in Thibet, which gives one just the same effect of a cliff created by human hands. The adjective is "Toppling."

Such a height was very well chosen by Fate for the episode which most distinguishes it in history, or at least which is best remembered by the foreign traveller who has some smattering of Bohemian history. For it was from a window in this precipice of stone that the malcontents threw the Emperor's delegates to what should have been their death. These unpopular men went sailing through the air, and that would have been the end of them had they not lighted on a great heap of manure piled up against the last courses of the castle wall. The accident saved their lives, but not their dignity, and the whole affair became known as "the Defenestration of Prague."

"Defenestration" is an arresting word, and I am glad that it should have got its niche of permanent fame in the story of Europe. It means, of course, nothing more than "a throwing-out-of-the-window"—which indeed it was, and to some purpose! But it has a majesty about it, a roll and an emphasis, which you only get in connection with the august Latin tongue. There have been other defenestrations—I witnessed one or two myself as an undergraduate, and there was one, almost fatal, in Vienna only the other day. But in Prague was *The* Defenestration, and it will be a permanent warning to public men not to moot disputed questions in upper storeys. The Defenestration of Prague is worthy of being thus set apart and glorified, for it began the Thirty Years' War. It was the first act in that drama (not yet concluded, though many people think it is) wherein is played out the issue between the tribal and the centralised in mid-Europe.

The other monument in Prague which I shall always remember—over and above the famous bridge—is the huge modern statue of John Huss. I wonder what the present masters of the town have done with it! On the one hand, it is a protest against Germanism, on the other hand it is a protest against Rome. So both those who want to get rid of it and those who want to preserve it could use their own arguments on either side. I presume it still stands and will remain. It swears rather with its surroundings, for it is not only new but what is called "modern," while all about it is old. From the pile of faggots at Constance he uttered (or is said to have uttered) the famous phrase "Sancta Simplicitas." I know not how it be with others, but for my part those words have always endeared him to me.

Like every other main site in Europe, Prague has its geographical reason, as has Bohemia whereof it is the centre. The Bohemian quadrilateral is a square of mountain ranges, open on the south side, closed by walls of high hills to the east and west and north. Through this last barrier, the northern one, the Elbe cuts its way before the beginning of human record. A deep narrow gorge winds for miles, confining the river to its course and leading from the open country on the Bohemian side to the open country on the German. I suppose the whole formation rose like many another such (that to the north of Alsace, for instance), through the damming up of the main stream by a barrier of high land causing above it a lake, thence an outlet by a waterfall, and that waterfall cutting the gorge backwards, till it was even all along. Or perhaps it was a natural fissure which the river borrowed. These questions are for the geologists, not for me. And when I come to think of it, the gorge cannot have been made in that fashion at first, for the river here flows from south to north. Had the gorge been cut by a waterfall, as Niagara has cut its way back, it would have had to have started in the north and worked southward.

In whatever way it was formed, the gorge of the Elbe made the entry into Bohemia difficult; it gave it isolation and defence, and preserved the original nomads who settled there, so that they could form a State. The Moldau, before it fell into the Elbe, watered the plain and made it fertile. On its banks in the centre of the quadrilateral, the natural converging place and market of that enclosed garden, rose Prague.

In what phase of its thousand years of history do we stand now? No man can conceivably say, and they that are loudest in their affirmations know least. But this much is sure: of necessity, from the mere structure of the land, Prague will command Bohemia, and Bismarck repeated an ancient truth when he said "He who holds Bohemia holds mid-Europe."

Portugal

LAST SUMMER THERE WAS HELD A COMMEMORATION IN Portugal of the country's political origins under its first king.

I should have thought that a better initial date, if one had to stake down such a thing, would be the granting of local government to Henry of Burgundy whose father-in-law, the king of Castile and Leon, had set him up as Count over what is now the northern part of the country between the Minho and the Tagus, or rather the approaches to that river. But it was not till the time of Henry's son, forty-five years later, that the term 'Count,' which connoted subordination to a feudal superior, became 'king,' the distinctive title all over Christendom for the head of the independent government. Indeed, Portugal might serve as an example of what a peculiar spiritual value attached to the word and office of Rex. I defy any man to make his way through the labyrinth and to say why that tangled undergrowth of feudalism produced in one place the beginning of the national unity in the shape of kingships and in another no more than the title Count or Duke or Marquis. So far as real independence goes, a Duke of Normandy was as much his own master and the master of all the countries he administered as was that other aspect of the same man, the King of England. I fancy the real force at work was the "Magic of The Word."

Anyhow, something did it and what did it we don't know. Whatever it was, it lay at the root of the great Capetan story; for the Kings of France became what they were and gathered the country round them into a unity through the magic of their title, certainly not through the material force of their arms. Out of the word "king" came the modern nation, which modern men worship and which is now in its turn challenged. And when the harbour district Oporto (which was also called by the double name Porto Calle) extended over the lands to the south of it, the name and title of these Burgundian princes, Portugal as a nation was born.

It did not know it was a nation, though I am afraid I shall offend a good many people by saying this; for men always read history backwards and no habit more distorts the story of mankind. But it became a nation slowly by reaction against the advancing Spanish power to the east; and the sense of political personality was vastly increased when, in the height of the great united Spanish monarchy, the union of the whole Peninsula was made. That act, which lasted but a lifetime, annealed or forged the already existing nation of Portugal—a nation which already had centuries behind it. It made of Portugal a powerfully conscious thing. Such it has remained through the most extraordinary risks and perils which ought at least twice, by any human calculation, to have swamped it; and with the same undercurrent which flowed through the making of all the other nationalities of the west, Portugal was driven.

It was no natural division, unless we may call it a sort of congeries built up from the navigable ocean reaches of the Spanish rivers; it is protected by no mountain chain. When you enter it from the north you pass what is now a true frontier but in all the feudal ages was no more than a local river. When you enter it from the east you pass through districts which are now and then isolated and barren, more commonly indistinguishable from the districts around. Yet this inward personality of the State which was to become, in the second part of the Christian era, a nation, took roots, strengthened and grew.

Englishmen ought to know Portugal well for there is a very important commercial bond between the two countries and there was for generations a still stronger political bond, the remainder of which can be felt even in the arrangements of modern Europe, even amid the dangers of general shipwreck through which modern Europe is now passing and in which the whole of Christendom is tossed as in a storm, through the abandonment of the traditions of Christendom.

But Englishmen do not know Portugal well. Some very few know it better than any other European country, but the bulk of English opinion and experiences, of English reading and of English travel, leaves Portugal to one side.

That is just as well, for as it has been said that the nation is happy which has no history, so it may be said that a nation is happier for having whatever history it possesses secured by a certain isolation from that of its neighbours. Everything should apparently have made Portugal more familiar to the English writer and traveller than any other part of the West, save, of course, that there was the gulf of religion. But the great harbour of Lisbon has meant so much to the fleet of England and the approach of English armies has, ever since the Middle Ages, so learnt the Portuguese countrysides that one would have thought that a sufficient tradition would have been created. It has not been so and that is a pity. It is especially a pity because there is one thing about Portugal which particularly makes the country feel attuned to the English mind, and that is the influence of the sea.

If there is one slice of Christendom, one portion of Europe which was made by the sea more than another, Portugal is that slice, that portion, that belt. Portugal was made by the Atlantic.

You see that influence in the highly characteristic architecture so especially national, called the Manuelesque. Its elaboration disturbs the purist; and the devout lover of our Gothic, which sprang from the north-centre of France, arising in the districts of Paris and of Chartres, is sometimes bewildered, more often shocked, by Manuelesque extravagance in porch or window-frame. But look closely at the thing and you will see that it is a creation of the ocean and the ocean's inhabitants, human and other. Hence everywhere the motive of the cable: The Manuelesque architecture is founded on the rope and the knot. Hence also that sinuosity, that undulation which contrasts so strongly with the mathematical rigidity of the northern Gothic and also with the majestic arch and column and dome of the Renaissance. In the crannies of Manuelesque ornament you even get the little beasts of the sea and it is not extravagant to say that when you have, perhaps with some difficulty, made yourself so familiar with the style as to have an appetite for it and to respect it, you will whenever you come upon it, and you only come upon it in this land, feel the surge of the Atlantic and feel that vast air.

Lisbon

WHAT WILL BE THE FUTURE FORTUNES OF LISBON, I wonder? We are approaching the mid-twentieth century. We are in the midst of a world very rapidly changing in its strategics as in everything else. We are confused by our memories and traditions of the older state of things which the coming of machinery had already begun to transform a lifetime ago and which is now manifestly in process of dissolution and replacement.

What Lisbon meant in the older state of things we all know. It has been called, in recollection of the English connection with Portugal and of the gradual English extension of sea power, "the key of the Mediterranean." For that magnificent harbour, though it is far from the Mediterranean entrance and faces the Atlantic, is a natural base for operations in the Mediterranean on the part of anyone who controls the Straits which are the gates of that sea.

For, indeed, the harbour of Lisbon, is one of those exceptional opportunities which political geography now and then presents—but rarely. The world is full of deep and convenient and sheltered harbours. Calm fiords running inland, and with anchorage in their upper reaches at least, even though they be too deep in the neighbourhood of the sea; such profound inlets as the eastern coast of the Adriatic abounds in, or such as the long bays of the southwestern coast of Ireland, or the whole western seaboard of

Scandinavia. But these natural harbours have an irritating way of standing in places where there is no corresponding use for them in commerce or in transport. They serve barren or ill-populated lands. That is especially remarkable in the Adriatic, where all the rich Lombard plain and all the flat fertile land served by the Emilian Way, to the east of the Apennines, has but one true natural refuge (put indeed to the highest use historically), where the lagoon of Venice is, with one other originally only half-sheltered "hook" of land at Ancona; while, opposite those fertile lands and those wealthy cities which crowd northern Italy, you have, beyond the Adriatic sea, completely sheltered havens in profusion and no one to use them.

Now Lisbon, merely as a harbour, is one of the best conceivable. The entry is neither too narrow nor too broad: about a mile and a quarter across from the point of Fort Bugio on the southern, to the point of Fort St. Julian on the northern side. The bar has never been an obstacle, though it now has to be dredged for the largest modern ships; one passes it in seven fathoms of water in the central point at low spring tides, and once within the narrows of the mouth there extends a great landlocked sheet of water, seven miles long by two to seven at its broadest part; much of the southern part is shoal, but in the main channel a whole fleet can ride. It is the estuary of the Tagus.

With that unerring sense for maritime opportunity which developed in England under the Stuarts (who made the British Navy and fixed its form), the rapidly growing commercial and financial power of England fixed upon the Portuguese alliance and therefore, in time, upon the use of Lisbon. From the beginning of the eighteenth century the alliance of England as a sea power with Portugal and her great harbour continued unchecked. The rivals of

England sneered at Portugal as a mere dependency; they sometimes called it a "colony" of this country. But the connection was of ample service to the Portuguese nation. The benefits were mutual and remained so uninterruptedly until those late revolutionary days in which all things are changing. The lines of Torres Vedras are of first class importance in the military history of this country. They count far more in the story of the struggle with the French Empire than do any of the actions in the war of movement after those defensive lines had ceased to exercise their original functions, for it was the lines of Torres Vedras that preserved the use of Lisbon Harbour.

Well, what will the future do with that magnificent site? To what purpose of naval strategy will it be attached, if any? Some future fortunes it must have, though these may not be the fortunes of fighting by sea or by land. But some new rôle it must play. What?

I deliberately leave that note of interrogation to stand by itself without putting on too many airs of pretending to the beginning of a solution, for if ever there were a case of no man knowing the future, this is one. The splendid harbour of Lisbon is there with certain obvious attributes and functions attaching to it. We cannot predicate how those attributes and functions will be used, but we can at least enumerate them. It is a manifest base, whether for attack upon, or defence of, the entry into the Mediterranean. It lies on the flank of all that premier trade route of the modern world, the steamship lanes converging round the corner of Capes Cabo and Finisterre and thence swinging round southward.

Nothing is more striking when one takes the journey to Lisbon by sea than to look westward from the decks and note the frequency of shipping passing before one on the seaward side, north and south, as one approaches the corner of the land. There go the ships to and from the Garonne, the Elbe and the Weser, the Thames, the Seine and the Scheldt, the ships from the Baltic, the ships from Amsterdam and from the issues of the Rhine. Every ship for the South African seas or for the Orient, through Suez, comes swinging round that elbow of land. So does every ship coming home to the great northern merchant ports, to London and Copenhagen and Gothenburg, Rotterdam and Cherbourg: all of them.

Lisbon, lying thus on the flank of the converging trade routes, remains of equal importance, whether the Mediterranean be open or closed, whether the Suez Canal be denied to one or the other belligerent, or maintain its neutrality.

It is a general rule in history that the expected rarely happens. But let every man who cares for reality and knows the meaning of a chart study the position of that famous land-locked sheet and remember that the earlier meaning of the place may return at any moment, although on behalf of what cause we can none of us tell. One possibility out of many must be borne in mind. Lisbon may yet once more become, and that in the near future, the centre of a great trade, and arise as a major maritime capital of Western Europe.

The Tagus

I WONDER WHETHER THE TAGUS, THE RIVER TAGUS, WILL appear again suddenly, familiarly, in our speech here in the North. It has played a very great part in history, and one point of it—where it meets the ocean—a leading part. But it is the good fortune of the river that even widely travelled men have for the most part no familiar acquaintance with its course. They come upon it here and there, usually at one of two crossings only, and for the rest, have no experience of it. I myself who am writing this have never travelled down the full length of the valley nor anything like it. I know part of the last section where it runs through Portugal to the Atlantic; I know it near its sources; I have known it well and frequently where it rushes round Toledo in a great horseshoe bend, which might almost be called a gorge.

Where it struck me most, the reach that still remains most permanently in my memory, for it is the most characteristically Spanish of all, is that magnificent deserted sweep of land, a grand depression in Central Spain; so sweeping that it seems almost shallow, though it is hundreds of feet from the rim to the river: the place where the Tagus divides Estremadura, and where the great highroad, now so well kept and modernised, the backbone of Western Spain, the link joining Seville to Burgos, crosses the yellow Tagus by the bridge between Carceres and Plasencia. In that landscape you have the very heart of Spain, the marriage of wide uplands with wide and empty skies; the yellow, friable earth; the half-deserted land. It is almost the landscape of Africa, but nobler than Africa, nobler than anything that I have seen in the Atlas or in the lift of the lands above the Tell beyond the hill-villages of the Kabyles.

There, on that bridge, a man might pause and contemplate at his leisure, establishing communion between his own soul and the world of the Spaniards. It sounds almost blasphemous to say so, but I contend, advance the idea, that one is nearer the very heart of Spain in these cups as large as a county, framed in and held by their distant mountain rims, than one is even in the presence of what man himself has best done in Spain—the miracle of Seville, the miracle of the Chapel Royal at Burgos, the splendour of Salamanca seen from beyond/ the river, towering above the bridge and the town. All these places and twenty more must have their separate description from me if I am to show due gratitude for having known them, but still I should desire to express most gratitude for that vision of the central Tagus valley, empty of men, filled with the gods—but the gods of a hard, peculiar land.

The Spanish landscape, particularly in these stretches of it whence man is almost absent, gives out an impression of endurance as does nothing else I know. One says to oneself: The well watered countries of the North have changed perpetually and are changing before our eyes today, the men of the north riot in experiment, triumph, failure, achievement and failure again. The desert also beyond the sea, beyond Atlas, is utterly unchanging, but unchanging after a different fashion, for no man seeks a habitation there nor thinks of it in terms of a mortal polity. But Spain—these great steppes of Spain—have something of both the changing and the unchanging, and yet resemble neither. It is land habitable enough and breeds famous races of men. From this very countryside of which I speak here came certain of the mighty Conquistadores, the like of whom was never known before their time or has been known since, riders of horses and dominators of the world.

Here also, if one knows where to find them, are the castles of old time, not yet in ruins yet more than half abandoned. Here are the rare lesser habitations of men, seeming to take the colour of their walls from the colour of the burnt earth around them. No, it is not an inhuman land, nor one whence men flee, as is the desert, yet it is not a land wherein men can consider comfort and consumption and sink in ease. It is everywhere a land of challenge, and, what is more, a land provoking worship of something symbolised by those wave-like mountainsides.

Indeed, these sweeps of the bare Iberian land, almost treeless, almost untenanted, resemble and recall the sea, but a sea upon a scale more than titanic, a sea moved by gales such as our world never knows.

I have read of a man who went all the way down the Tagus in a boat, like that other man who went all down the still more formidable Amazon shortly after the white man first came there. The man who went all the way down the Tagus in a boat did so during the reign of Philip II, when Portugal and Spain were under one Crown. There was an idea that the Tagus could be used for traffic, locked, perhaps canalised, made navigable at least from Toledo to the sea, and perhaps this man made the experiment in his boat to test the value of the scheme. Nothing came of it. The Tagus is still unbridled; it keeps the grandeur of savage things, when those things remain free from cages and the domination of man.

I wonder whether any man has put up a monument to the Tagus in verse? I am far too ignorant to know of such myself, or even to tell by hearsay whether such a poet and poem there be. If it has not been done, I recommend the task to any rhymester of any country, but best of all to some genius of Estremadura. He should put more of battle and of fixity, of foundation, more of a sombre divinity, more also of persistent energy in what he had to say of the Tagus than could be possible with any other theme. It is a conceit of mine that rivers, being each under the protection of its own Numen, each having (in a word) a soul, take pride in praise and recognise their laudators, and most of all their poets. I certainly hope it is so, for that would make mankind less lonely. He has fellowship indeed with rivers, has man: he should be grateful for that gift; but how pleasing it would be to receive a recognition of the bond! To describe such a vision, the meeting between a mortal and the greater River-gods would need among English pens the pen of Mr Algernon Blackwood, as you may see if you will read his book "The Centaur." I know not whether he be familiar with the Tagus or no, but let any man who would exalt his own name by written worship of that river get his inspiration from Mr Blackwood's tale. Therein also you have a veiled vision of the gods.

Spain

Those who write today on the theme of any one country in Christendom are haunted by the knowledge that their theme is uncertain. The subject which they desire to treat is not sufficiently fixed in the dimension of time. Anyone writing or speaking to the text "France," "England," "Ireland" remembers even as he begins to think of his matter that that matter is changing. Can he securely speak of an England, a France, an Ireland which even an immediate posterity shall recognise? We predicate of any one province of Christendom that it is thus and thus, but even as we make the affirmation the condition we take for granted may be changing—such is the peculiar misfortune, but also the peculiar interest of the time in which we live.

For instance, had I for my theme "England" (and that was a theme on which I wrote my best three years ago in a little book wholly devoted to the nature and probable fate of England), I would affirm as a matter of course, as something recognised by the whole world and something necessarily enduring, a nation, the chief mark of which was unity. Alone, I would say, and did say, of England: "This country is free from internal strain of any kind." It enjoys a complete similarity of substance throughout because it has but one religion, but one official history which everyone is taught, but one object of worship, the nation itself. I would affirm that this unity was as enduring as granite. But in some few years that affirmation might prove out of date. The character one affirms as a matter of course may have ceased to be. For this unity of England is a function of her aristocratic political structure where everything works within the frame of class government and of generation after generation during which civil disturbance and foreign armies within English soil have been completely forgotten. But a reverse of military fortune, an invasion, or even only a grave defeat would destroy that mood for ever, and as for class government, there are already indications that this apparently unchangeable English thing is in some ways subtly undermined. In my own lifetime, I have witnessed the change in meaning of the word "gentleman," and still more the change in political function implied by that word.

If the idea of change thus haunts every man professing to speak of a modern nation, if that idea be so omnipresent that it applies even to England, how can one make certain that in speaking of any other group in Christendom one can predicate continuity of spirit and action, and constant similarity to itself.

How, above all, can one postulate these things in connection with the word "Spain"? For my part, as a completely foreign observer, but one with a profound attachment to this thing which I have observed, I am certain of that self similarity, of that individual soul and personality, which gives the word "Spain" its meaning.

But I can well understand anyone less profoundly moved by that very word, or less experienced through travel with the unity underlying the variety of Spain, marvelling that anyone should consider that unity as a certitude: marvelling that anyone could speak of a general European task falling to Spain and Spain alone, of any European rôle especially and exclusively Spanish. "Look," you would say, "what this word 'Spain' has meant within living memory: the Civil Wars, of which the last and most terrible is but now concluded, the unparalleled diversity of provincial life, including one province, the wealthiest, with a highly differentiated tongue, Catalan, and another with language and social traditions unique and wholly apart from the rest: the Basque." You might go on to say: "The historical development of the Peninsula has made unity impossible. The kingdoms spreading in strips from the North during the progress of the Re-conquest from Islam could never amalgamate save mechanically. They might obey one Crown, but their roots were separate. So true is it that one of them, Portugal, actually became an independent State and one which fiercely affirmed its private character, and re-affirmed it after amalgamation for a lifetime with the rest of Peninsular things."

Or he might add, might the critic who should doubt the unity of that theme "Spain," "Look at the violent physical contrasts imposed by nature herself, the alternative oven-breath of high summer upon the plateau and the icy arctic winds that sweep the same plains for half the year: the garden, as it is so well called, which fringes the Mediterranean and the solemn, arid steppe of the inland height: the earth, which made our fathers speak of the Iberian land as 'dura tellus,' something which, for a very texture of hardness, is not to be matched anywhere in the West. Look at the transformation of landscape upon which a man gazes. The moment he has crossed the middle Pyrenees and comes upon the central marches of the Ebro, see how one parallel mountain chain after another cuts off region from region and forms of each countryside something special and separate.

"If that were not enough for dissipation of unity, consider the two main facts of all Spanish history since the conversion of the Empire. First, the Mohammedan tide swirling up to and over the Pyrenees, next the long ebb thereof which will always be known as the Re-conquista wherein the true Middle Ages were born: wherein the Gothic and the Universities and the vernacular epics and the chivalric spirit welled up for the remaking of Europe. There is not a town from the edges of Navarre to the extreme South which has not seen the advent, the presence and the retirement of Mohammedan administration, which has not heard the singsong of the Koran in its schools and heard that echo die out. How can you fuse into one a double inheritance so deeply contrasted?"

All this is true; but meanwhile, a certain other spirit moves over this unearthly land. That other spirit which imposes unity, gives its meaning to the word "Spain."

Let us feel it first physically as it is in landscape and in the feel of the air, and next consider it at work everywhere in the works of man.

The Spanish Air

PHYSICALLY, THOUGH THE SPANISH CLIMATE PASSES FROM an oceanic to a Mediterranean zone, the two not divided by any natural boundary merging one into the other, Spain is one: or rather, the Peninsula is one, for though Portugal is a separate State from the rest and has vigorously founded and defended its independence, Portugal also is in its historical origins and development only one of its fellow-Iberian sectors. It grew gradually by conquest southwards, as did its neighbour, Castile, and Aragon also and beyond that Valencia. Portugal, also, is steeped, like the rest of the Peninsula, in the effect of the long crusading battle which re-established Christendom south of the Pyrenees and ultimately purged Western Europe of Islamic influence. Lisbon, the great central harbour, whereon Portugal was formed, was Mohammedan in government right into the twelfth century. But allowing for the political exceptions of Portugal, the Peninsula is one and Spain is certainly one.

Now, that unity which has made Spain a nation and must always keep it a nation, is not mainly physical; and the spiritual thing you feel at once after you have passed the Pyrenees. The influence comes more gradually, of course, along the eastern border where the Catalan race and language and social tradition overlap the mountains. The Roussillon is Catalan and even to-day, after three centuries of unison with the French State, the Roussillon is Catalan. Perpignan is a French town right enough. It is French in its architecture, in its general speech and in its political traditions, but there is something about it which is particular and local. Perpignan does not look southward. No one living there long can forget the connection between Perpignan and Catalonia beyond the border.

This unity of Spain, this spiritual unity may be compared to a colour and that colour is the colour of gold. But it is gold shot with a certain blazonry of more various hues. There is a sort of gorgeousness in the historic colour of Spain which has been compared to the gorgeousness of the Western sky at sunset. This influence, for which colour is the best metaphor, spreads wherever the Spanish tongue and the Spanish social system has impressed itself. The Conquistadores came and told, the first and boldest of them from Estremadura. Now Estremadura, though it is not central, remains in the memory, I think, of most foreigners who have traversed it, the most Spanish of Spanish land. Those huge billows of bare slopes, rising into the crested foam as it were of the mountain ranges, the splendid loneliness of those empty sweeps demand and obtain their habitation by an unseen company, which company is the ancestry of Spain.

But everywhere it is the same story, whether you regard the lonely grandeur of this frontier province or the crannies of the ultimate high valleys which overhang the fringe of the Mediterranean plain, or the old walled towns of the North, Avila, the Roman walls and towers of Leon, there hangs over all those landscapes an effect of enchantment, a sense of things beyond this world. Even the dullest have felt this sharply with any one of the great shrines, but in time all men feel it. I cannot myself, after so much wandering about on foot and in silence during the years when I was still free to travel thus, pick out one place more than another as being especially haunted by the genius of Spain, but you feel that spirit, something wholly itself and as different from the rest of Europe as a vision from the light of common day in all shrines—and more especially in their darkness.

Thus if any man tell you that Barcelona, because it is Catalan, is not also Spanish, go into the Cathedral coming out of the blazing sun and look with your back to the Coro at the mystery of the eastern nave with the Crucifix of Lepanto permanently inspiring the gloom. I say "stand thus and gaze in this fashion," but I am talking in terms of my middle life and of years ago. I have not seen Barcelona since the wars.

Nor have I seen Huesca wherein I first, in my youth, came upon the Gothic stonework of Aragon. I know not whether there will remain the time, the opportunity to linger once more and fully at peace in those cities which so strongly affected me half a lifetime ago, of which I visited the last while the civil conflict was still raging, but that they will be restored to all their ancient spirit, and that others, at least, will be transformed, as I have been in my time by their magic, that I take to be certain.

For when the victory was won, so brief a time ago, it was won for good. It was the most complete, the most perfect achievement. Not only Spain re-arose as a light is re-lit on a tower, but that Christendom, of which she was the champion and the symbol, was also restored. It is a great thing to have lived in such a time, although the full meaning of the time will not be seen by the men of my generation.

There is no doubt that the tide in Europe has turned and it turned, I repeat, when the decision was successfully taken to engage in the hard battle for the recovery of the lower Ebro bank. The calculation seemed perilous, but it proved just. When I stood in that high mountain village (the headquarters of an army) as the guest for a moment of one of Spain's most famous soldiers, when I looked below me to that battle landscape in which, as in all modern battle landscapes, one saw hardly any movement, in which the masses of men were hidden and not even cannon smoke announced, as it would have announced when I was young, the struggle proceeding; when I heard the news of the successive retirement of the revolutionaries eastward upon the hills which lay between me and the sea, I did not know, even then so late, that the thing had been accomplished and Europe saved. Yet so it was.

A keen wind blew out of the distant Pyrenean heights which lay, very clear-cut in snow and shade, against the intense blue of the frozen sky. In such an air all, on to the most distant ridges of the west, stood out in intense clarity. The whole thing had an effect as of something instantaneous: fixed in a flash and intended as a symbol of permanence. And so it was. The thing had been accomplished and I had assisted at its accomplishment. I can never be sufficiently grateful for this.

On an Etching

There is a picture which constantly returns to my mind. It represents that very fine thing the Royal Palace at Madrid, seen from the riverside looking up from the east bank of the Manzanares: the older palace, which was the Alcazar of the town and the special residence of the kings of Castille. That has, of course, been replaced by the also very fine eighteenth-century palace, which still stands and was built after the first had been burnt a little before the middle of the eighteenth century. The etching (for it is an etching) is stamped with the spirit of the time and might be from the hand of Isaac Sylvestre, whose style it closely resembles. I will take that picture for my text, a text of a commonplace sort but one to which it is wise to return: the vicissitude of human affairs.

No generation has, of course, any conception of what will come after it, not even of what will come immediately after it; and that is one of the reasons why it is so difficult to write history, because it is so difficult to remember that the men of any particular time had no conception of what *we* know upon their future. If there was one thing that seemed permanent in the moment when that etching was made it was the Spanish Monarchy. The date of engraving is 1707, which is a good deal later (writing from memory) than Isaac Sylvestre, but the touch is there and it seems to be of his school. But that is a detail on which I need not delay you.

At any rate, there stands the fine great building with the stamp of political permanence upon it. The mere material evidence disappeared, but the manner in which it was replaced was proof of the spiritual strength on which it was founded. Men could not think that such a political edifice as the Imperial House of Spain, its absolute powers, its vast dominions, could change, let alone disappear. In a sense, indeed, it has not done so. The Spanish temper is the most enduring thing in Christendom. It seems to be made of harder material than any other. It is fitting, therefore, that it should never admit Lost Causes. What it has done, even in the remote past, it does today and will do again for perhaps another thousand years. Cast your mind over those two centuries and more since that etching was made and consider the fortune of the place and of its people. How enormous were the waves of change.

All men could see that the once unchallengeable power of the sixteenth-century Spain had waned; all men had begun to regard the phase of that time in which the drawing was made as a phase of long and very slow majestic decline, though a decline none the less. But what no one could conceive, what no one in fact did conceive, was that catastrophic storm could burst against that rock. Yet before the sons of those who looked on this edifice during the wars of the Spanish succession were dead, the Empire was in fragments, the Colonies had broken away, fierce invasions had tortured the very soul of the people (and had called forth still more fierce resistance), the immemorial religion had been challenged and was to be threatened with uprooting. It is true that Spain remained more itself than any other province of Christendom, centred round its hard core of great bare uplands, alternately frozen and ablaze with the violence of the torrid sun. But even Spain shook in that mighty wind which had arisen at the Revolution to sweep all Europe.

Men who regret the past (that is, nearly all men who know what the past was), will perpetually strive in spirit if not in action to restore the lost thing even as it was, even in its particular ornaments and adjuncts. Therefore it is hopeless as we all know though not futile, for if it were not made the surrender would mean the spirit of man had accepted the challenge of time, and if the spirit of man were to accept the challenge of time it would have abdicated: it would have lost its sovereignty. No, we do not restore the past because we cannot; but by a desperate effort to restore it we maintain the continuity of life. See how abject, how despicable, are all things which boast that they are wholly new; that they owe nothing to tradition. See how lacking they are in sap. How tasteless and often how insane.

There is, of course, one awful and sacred plot of that hard Iberian land which bears, more than any other, this mark of endurance: I mean the Escorial. I have written of it too often to write again of it here. But I salute it: the supreme monument of human permanence in stone, the supreme symbol of majesty. For the Escorial is one of those names which, even as one writes it down, compels reverence. In time it must at last be gone as must for that matter, the Pyramids; but it seems to me that works of this mighty sort are like dents inflicted on the armour of time and proving in our struggle against the all-devouring enemy that we shall ultimately be his masters. But not here.

When I consider how side by side with the divine constructive effort of the human race there runs a spirit of mere destruction, I find it the most incomprehensible department in all the problem of evil. There arise among men negative demands, a sort of appetite for ruin, which roars to be satisfied. Ruin through the gradual effect of nature makes no such assault upon the soul of man as does this insane business of killing and tearing down and laying waste. The gradual operation whereby things return to that from which they came has about it something almost of repose. It is inevitable and in the nature of things. All human creation of wealth is something done against the tide: something which is of necessity ultimately doomed. But this lust for undoing, this sort of anarch boast is, I say, incomprehensible on any scheme of philosophy tenable by a sane man.

Yet there it is, perpetually recurrent in history, a menace never altogether repelled, a brute never wholly or finally tamed. It feels it to be no rebuke but a sort of glory that it should be impotent in every art, save the art of murder, moral or material. Its victims are its trophies and the more noble that which is killed the greater its triumph.

In all the human story there stands at the beginning of each new chapter the heroes, who are also after a fashion gods. These were not exalted nor their names made immortal by courage alone, but by the object of the struggle against which the courage was deployed. They conquered the barbarian and the beast.

Burgos

I AM AFRAID FEW WILL AGREE WITH ME WHEN I SAY THAT, for myself, Burgos is the typical city of Spanish travel; but (as they say in the examination papers of the Universities) I will give "reasons for my answer."

At first sight that answer would seem insufficient. Seville is architecturally more glorious. Any one of the great ports is more alive with the sort of vitality which a visitor from the Northern Countries can understand. What must have been one of the chief pleasures of the town, the original glass of the Cathedral, has gone, and apart from the Cathedral no one outstanding monument symbolises the place.

Nevertheless Burgos remains for me the typical city because it is the typical frontier city of the successive waves of advance against the Mohammedan and because from it as you advance southward and westward you gradually grow in acquaintance with the particular land whence the expansion of Spanish culture spreads. For those who are called in Spanish story by the special name of the "Conquerors" were men of Estremadura. It has been ill-naturedly said of these heroes, as it has been said here in Britain of the Scotch, that they are driven to emigrate by the ingratitude of their native fields. But there is a far more profound root to the affair than either the distance or the infertility of Estremadura. With its people, as with the

Scotch, distance from a centre and lack of original natural wealth in the days when all was agricultural bred adventurers. Now all the story of mankind, at least all the story worth telling, is the story of migration, conquest, discovery, adventure.

But to return to Burgos. Burgos and adventure are bound up with the title of Estremadura. Why do I couple that title with the name of Burgos as a starting-point although the whole world of Old Castile lies in between. It is because a piece of personal experience links up for me the one with the other. It was from Burgos that I set out southward and westward as a young man and felt my way still southward and westward till I came to and crossed the Sierra. I have now almost forgotten that road save for here and there an intensely vivid picture and the magic of a name—in particular "The name of the Bridge" an Arabic name Alcantra. How well I recall my curiosity in those days of my ignorance (which is not yet much dispelled) to find this Arabic name far out upon the west of Christendom and well below the central line of Spain! I had first known it in Africa where you find those syllables attached, the Oriental word, to I know not how many river crossings.

Burgos also stands in my mind for the last of one crusading effort and the beginning of another. It was the capital of the Advance planted in the debatable belt across which that Advance was made. But I am afraid no one will get that emotion of a crusading memory who comes into Burgos as pretty well everybody has to by the railway. Let anyone who only knows that unfortunate form of entry get out at any small station up the line and make his way on foot into Burgos. Then I think he may know what I mean.

Burgos typifies also what is another characteristic of

Spain and that is the endless fertility of architectural adventure: the flowering of stone. You get it everywhere, of course. But you get it here all the more strongly set because the colour of glass is lacking and because the countryside you have been traversing hardly prepares you for so different a thing.

One feature about Burgos I do regret and that is the twin spires. I cannot explain why they seem to me out of tune with the air of the place: why they seem to me adventitious. They are old enough to know better. But I do believe that if you were to show a man for the first time a photograph of those twin spires taken from far away enough to lose the detail, and to ask him what province of Christendom they belonged to, the last guess he would make would be "Spain." Whereas were you to show any man not wholly barbaric and benighted the soaring Tower of Seville and ask him what it was, he would at once and certainly utter the name and proclaim the glory of Spain.

I trust that Burgos will forgive me these very few words and remember how much I love her, glass or no glass, spires or no spires. Also Burgos has given me very good food in a very good hotel to which I now and here renew my homage. It showed this kindness to an unknown wayfarer who will always keep it in mind. Burgos receives its guest. It is not too proud to do so in spite of its enormous history and of its incredible Royal Chapel.

As I write thus at random about Burgos—and bringing into those few lines too much irrelevant matter—I am moved to consider the whole problem of presenting to others any personal experience of foreign tours.

There are many ways of tackling that problem and I have myself approached it from all sorts of angles. I can only give my own preferences in the matter and leave them for the reader to accept or to reject at his pleasure.

What I take to be the very worst form of travel talk or travel writing is the guide-book form. It is a necessary form. We could not get on without it. Any properly equipped literature must include great masses of mere detailed summaries upon foreign places even though these catalogues are often at the best a mere ladder of names and at the worst a mere repetition of false and hackneyed judgements. But I take it that travel talk at the other extreme of that category, I mean wholly personal experiences, the unadorned statement of what struck the individual observer most, especially when he first visited some foreign scene, is the most useful of all.

When I first began that kind of thing I was terrified of inaccuracy. Inaccuracy is the bogey of all young writers. I suppose that is because they are too fresh from their memories of examinations, in which odious activities accuracy is the only thing that counts. It is well, of course, that the guide-book style should be accurate but I take it that in travel talk as literature, that is as food for the spirit of man, accuracy is worth no more than the east wind or a packet of dust.

The more living, and therefore the more valuable of writers, even of writers on detailed history, have neglected accuracy because they despised it or because they had something better to do than waste their time on continual reference. I remember lecturing once, it must be thirty years ago at least, to a hall full of people even more ignorant than myself on the Acre of the Crusades and calling it Tyre from beginning to end. There was no harm done whether I called the place Tyre or Utopia; it was all one since neither I nor those who heard me had, at the moment, any experience of the Syrian coast.

What a writing man should set down about his travels is what he saw or thought he saw, heard or thought he heard, and above all whatever struck him with the shaft of beauty.

It is his business to furnish his reader's mind. I hope that Coleridge (or whoever it was) never bothered about Kubla Khan (if that is the way to spell the gentleman's name); I am certain that he never bothered about the Sacred River Alph or looked it up in an atlas. He would have been a great fool if he had, for there is, I suppose, no such stream and it is quite unimportant whether there be one or no. Coleridge created it in a piece of trebly immortal verse as quintessentially distilled as the best of Armagnac—which is saying a great deal. It was his business to create, not to describe.

It is true that if in your travel talk you say things that are too outrageous altogether you will earn a reputation of a liar. But a man who is ashamed of that reputation had better not touch on travel at all.

One of the men who has pleased me most, writing in the late Middle Ages, said of a fantastic tree growing in some foreign part that it produced by way of fruit "little lambs . . . But they have no wool."

I call that charming. That is the kind of tree I want to read about. I can do without the wool; if I want real wool I can go and get some in a shop. But in what shop can I buy the fruits of Fairyland? I think it was the same writer who assures us that in some place he visited there were men whose faces grew below their necks in the middle of their chests. I hope there are. I hope to come across them. But lacking such amusement the lie will serve well enough. Whether there be such men or no it is enough to have heard of them. After all, all national history is a pack of lies, some of them quite outrageous and I think they are the better for being easily found out.

I remember a very acid man, a compatriot, therefore,

saying once at a large dinner to a man who had been holding forth profusely upon the wickedness of the Irish: "Pray, Sir, have you ever been to Ireland?" Whereat the worthy Extravagant answered cheerfully, "No, Sir! Nor have I any intention of going there; as you may guess from what I have just been saying." It was a complete and final answer: granted, of course (I repeat) that the cheerful romancer didn't mind being called a liar.

It is perhaps the first lesson in courage which a man must learn if he wants to record his travels that even voluntary error is infinitely better than dullness. And as for involuntary error no one can write a page of description or history without falling into it head over ears.

The Twin Soul of Spain

I HAVE HESITATED LONG BEFORE GIVING THIS PAGE A TITLE. IT deals with something to which it is indeed difficult to give a name. For though that Something is of the highest importance and it is indeed known to all of us, yet a name has never been given it—save now and then some morbid pseudo-scientific name which did not fit the high case in point.

That case is the undoubted truth that in societies, as in individuals, there is not only commonly some diversity of will, but some duality of nature. It is foolish, and typical of a modern foolishness, to call that business "double personality," for that is just what it is not. When it becomes double personality it is so abnormal as to be out of the picture. On the contrary it is this duality of will or of character *within* the unity which the word "person" connotes that is the essence of the problem. In its simplest form there is the common struggle within the same soul between the good and the evil will, of which the individual mind is fully conscious. But the thing ramifies into much more than that. It applies, I say, to whole societies, even more than to individuals, for in the dimensions and dynamic powers of a great society there is more room for such conflict. It is particularly noticeable of the great main national tempers into which Christendom has fallen in the process of its development, and especially since the disruption of our common religion, three to four hundred years ago.

Examples in other nations than the Spanish of what I here consider would occur, I think, to everyone of my readers. Consider how, among the French, a very quick and lucid intelligence is coupled with that very negation of intelligence, action by mere sympathy or according to the association of ideas rather than according to reason. Thus a Frenchman is anti-clerical, nine times out of ten, from a mere social reaction against irritant conditions. I am convinced that most of the recent eccentric but shrill protest in favour of the Spanish Reds by prominent Catholics in France has had no deeper root than an exasperation with the traditions of what is called the "Faubourg" quarter of Paris, south of the river. It needed but the meeting with a few dowagers, a few high Tory gentlemen, the now fading aristocratic traditions of the St. Germains talking loyal nonsense, to start a reaction of this kind, in those whom such exasperates. In the same way there are masses of the French peasantry who have voted for a Communist candidate because they were angry with rural wealth, especially when it was inherited by an ancient family. The same men would have taken up arms and have fought fiercely to have defeated any Communist organization which might pretend to command them and to touch their little farms. Yet they voted, if not directly Communist, at any rate for the Popular Front (and therefore for Communist candidates) merely by association of ideas.

We have a similar contrast here in England between the lethargy, the slow physical action, the guarded statement and the retarded conclusion, of the average Englishman, and his astonishing aptitude for physical exercises that need electrically quick decisions, immediate actions and exact correlation of muscular effort. That English soul, to which gesticulation is so repugnant and a flash of decision by impulse so alien and suspect, is the same soul which, in the national games and in the prominent work of England at sea, does all things with greater swiftness, accuracy and decision than any other mind in Europe. Or, consider the Scottish innate instinct for equality and the Scottish indifference, for now so long, to economic freedom and to the practical social equality of man through the enjoyment of well divided property. Nowhere has the industrial revolution (what we call today "Capitalism," with its semi-serfdom), gone further than in the great industrial towns of Scotland. If you talk to members of these communities, you observe how much more rooted they are in the conception of human equality than are, say, the few remaining yeomen of our own northern counties, their neighbours.

Now among the Spaniards this contrast *within* the national soul shows itself in a fashion which has often been labelled a contrast between the ascetic and the sensual. Such a label is not well-found. The contrast is of another and more profound kind, by far, than the common conflict between appetite and discipline. It is rather a contrast of two twin intensities: two intensities of apprehension and of desire: two visions; the one a vision of what can be gained through beatitude, the other of what can be gained immediately, not only through the senses, but through all the faculties of man. It is a contrast between the vision of something distant, ardently expected and confidently so, and the vision of a satisfaction here and now—including the satisfaction of revenge.

I say that this doubleness in the Spanish soul has been, of late, more vividly apparent both to the native and to the foreigner—at least to the foreigner who has sufficient knowledge to make his judgment worth having. These very lines I am writing have been provoked by one of the latest

essays on this very thing, a piece of most important Jesuit
writing which appeared in the chief Belgian Catholic re-
view. But it is a matter which will continually occupy
the intention and the pen of the thoughtful man who is
allied to Europe.

It is as though there were two souls in Spain, and yet
clearly there is but one soul, though it is a soul torn in
opposite directions and liable to fall through the excess of
its action to one camp or the other in the two main divisions of spiritual activity which ultimately become the
Good and the Evil.

Spain is the very native land of carnage and of the
saints. Of those who martyrise and those who are martyred.
That is, of those who fail in the main task of the Christian
virtues and of those who mightily succeed. Men speaking
of their own country, writing books upon their own country, in the idiom of Castile, have given these books titles
which sufficiently exemplify what I mean. One of the most
notable of these titles was drawn from the arena of the
bull ring—"Blood and Sand"—and, let it be observed,
chiefly, beyond all other characteristics of the Spanish
spiritual intensity, that it is thus always on the level of high
combat. It is never base; it never sinks to material things.
It flames on either side of the barrier. This inner conflict
of Spain is in the individual soul and within all her society.
It is a conflict of things at white heat on either side.

What cause shall we discover for this strange degree of
contrast, sharper and more effective, proceeding to greater
extremes than in any other place, than in any other tradition, than in any other blood?

It has been ascribed by not a few to that evident outward contrast between the tremendous bare plains of the
Peninsula, vast surfaces of open land as dark as iron or as
a stormy sky (and on either edge of such an arena of

desolation, desolate mountains, craggy against the Northern and Southern sky): it has been ascribed, I say, to the contrast between these steppes, burning in their brief summer, icy under the winter winds, the "Garden," as the Spaniards themselves call it, which skirts the Mediterranean, and lies beneath the highlands all around, caressed by warmer winds, the place of fruits and of music and of palaces made for pleasure, guarded by the snows that enhance the beauty of such scenes and their amenities. But though that physical contrast (which is the note of the Spanish landscape and which any who have experienced it must remember all their lives) is a good symbol and perhaps a condition of that double character whereof I here debate, it is not the cause. Nothing material is the cause of things so deeply rooted in the very core of being.

The cause has been sought in history. The Spaniard, we are told, was first battered and annealed and raised up again by the conquest of the Roman armies. He was next further forged, annealed and constructed by the great assault of Islam. He was further granted an experience which, for its violence and its duration, was unique in Europe, the Reconquest: the gradual pushing back of that spiritual invasion and the triumph of the faith, even in the last Moslem strongholds of the south-east. Such a history has undoubtedly done much to make Spain what it is, to give the Spanish character its hardness and its edge, to make it a sword and to give it a sword, yet it is not enough to account for the thing we see; for the thing we see at work even now and here before us is the hardly human struggle between those who would have destroyed the Christian past and those who are, please God, recovering it as we see them recovering it.

No, I think the cause is rather to be sought in this: there permanently lives a Spanish fierce intensity, a thing long anterior to the Roman conquest, anterior to the coming of the Christ, anterior to the shrines and the Crusades. There was a certain material, charged at a certain high voltage, ready there to react against any external influence: that material was Spain. There fell upon the men who had done things beyond the power of men in other lands the influence of the Faith.

Now that influence is everywhere *one*; but the material upon which it works is diverse with climate, with physical experience, with race, with historical accident. Under so powerful an influence (it is the most powerful known to men and has proved the most enduring and the most creative; it is the only one not mortal), the Spanish temper was prepared for the dualism of which I speak; just as their sun which scorches the empty plains and cracks their rocks, shines with an intense action in the intensely cold sky of winter above those high places, just as the same physical source of energy makes the contrast of frost and fire, so within the mind of Spain there has appeared under the flame of the Faith, every potentiality for plus and minus in every scale. For torture and for heroism under torture, for revenge and for heroic forgiveness, for isolation accepted and for communal work, for exaggerated violence under arms and in popular furies. When such fires of division (which are also fires of creation) are at work, the fruits thereof are of a quality consonant to that which bred them: mighty fruits of evil and of sanctity.

Hence, I think, the picture that has been presented to us in the last few years. Hence the drama, partly of misunderstanding, partly of exalted determination, partly of hatred, partly of devotion, which has been played out, and the glory of it; the glory fools have blasphemed.

Cagliari

I AM NOT SURE THAT I SHOULD PUT THE HEADING "CAGLIARI" to what I am here writing, for the truth is that this word has suggested to me much more than the town: indeed, an indefinite number of things branching out from the memories of that name, and the first of these is the undoubted truth that modern machinery and the concentration of economic effort combined have made entry by sea much more difficult than it was even half a lifetime ago.

I found when last I went to Sardinia—which was not yesterday—that there was only one point on the coast at which one could land by any ordinary method of travel from Africa, and this was Cagliari. It is so with much more frequented places than Sardinia. International travel gets focused on one or two points and there is no choice of entry except by these. In the old days of sail a traveller went from pretty well any port he might choose to pretty well any other. He was not tied to a particular line. He had wide choice of entry to any foreign country that gave upon the sea. The choice gradually got narrower and narrower; the big steamship lines made it difficult to use any transport but their own; and as that transport got organised into a few regular lanes alternative opportunities disappeared.

When I reached Cagliari I was not sorry that modern conditions, political as well as economic, had delivered me there like a bale of goods with no freedom of choosing another harbour, for Cagliari has most of the good we find in old-established towns when these towns are sufficiently isolated. It is everywhere built upon its own past, retaining its own past, and thereby it remains spiritually more alive than the big, crowded, international hives.

Cagliari is a hill town, towering above its waters and above the valley to the east of it. It climbs up by steps of building, as it were, to its cathedral, and has all the diversity of successive planes in its design and changing views as the height increases. That continuity with the past, which is its most admirable character, gives it the same civic colour and tone which you find in the better known Sicilian cities to the south and east of it, and in particular it shows the *strata* of political history, the layers of political experience, which are the mark of such cities.

You recognize in a statue, in a corner shrine, in a chance ornamented window, this and that section of the past; now the Spanish dominion, now Savoy. Moreover, as one nearly always discovers in the really old towns which have kept themselves continuous, the remote past is hidden. To get the impression of pagan antiquity or even of the Dark Ages, you must count on buildings which have not been disturbed. You get such impressions most vividly in towns that have been dead, or half-dead, for centuries. You get it most strongly of all in towns that only remain as ruins. The continuously living towns build and rebuild upon themselves, as it were, burying their own past and rebury- ing it continually. One effect of this is that continuously living towns live in what one may call "The day before yesterday." They are never too modern—but also they never become museum pieces. Cagliari is here true to type.

One effect, by the way, of this building over of the past

by successive generations is that the historians are left spinning guesswork, while in the ruined and dead towns they can be certain. There are exceptions, of course. London still clearly shows its old Roman framework, especially in some of its main ways, Oxford Street and the Edgeware Road and the Roman road that runs southwest from old London Bridge, through Streatham (which takes its name from that road) to Dorking, Pulborough and Chichester.

Paris is even more continuous than London. You can stand on the rise of ground just south of the Sorbonne and look, at evening, down a line of lights going directly north, down the hill, across the island and so to the North Gate; and your eyes follow the very trace of the main Roman highway through the city. But as a rule the older the town, if it has been continuously inhabited, the more difficult to trace the framework of its remote past.

Another matter which occupies the mind of the traveller in Cagliari is the passing loyalties and enthusiasms of man. To-day everyone is in a fit of worship addressed to his own people. He worships the nation or the State, which is a fashion of worshipping himself. Let us all agree that oneself is an excellent object of worship—well known, demanding no mysteries and displaying every sort of excellence. But a little time ago, quite a few generations ago, mankind was not paying attention to anything of the sort; it was paying attention to the dynasties inheriting right by descent and marriage; and before that mankind was especially concerned with conflict of religion—and so on.

It is a commonplace that we should all like to come to life again later on and see what had happened. I confess that my own chief interest in that future which I shall not enjoy or suffer would be to take an ironical pleasure in the disappearance of our modern enthusiasms and their replacement by manias utterly different. How amusing it would be to find the citizens of such and such a modern polity, who are to-day in a frenzy for the greatness and glory of their State, occupied in devoted service to something alien, or some new idol—Caesar, some little man with a funny hat surrounded by elaborate ceremonial. Or to find them engaged in some furious discussion upon matters we have either never heard of or only think of as remote and dead.

If a man were to live on through centuries and retain his memory (a thing impossible) what fun he would get out of the violent attachment to ephemeral things. How astonished would the modern striker in Marseilles be to find himself in the Marseilles of less than 200 years ago, and how astonished a man of not 200 years ago would be to find himself in the Marseilles of the old Provence without any attachment to the rest of Gaul; and how bewildered and disgusted would be the Greek colonist, with his strong city-organisation around his secure port, to find himself in the Marseilles of any date you like later than the second Carthaginian War.

It seems a shame to load all these random thoughts upon the back of the poor Cagliari. I will cease from the task, but I do not promise to abandon Sardinia. There is a great deal more to be said about that happy island, and very few people to say it.

Patmos

Some time ago I happened to be sailing down south along the eastern coast of the island of Patmos, which I had never seen before save once from a very long way off from the west. Now, being close at hand, I was able to appreciate it more exactly and to see how the high outline of the island leads up to the Monastery of St. John towards the summit.

We all speak of the great beauty these Ægean islands show; and so they do in general outline. That sea which is so heavenly of itself in colour and texture is made the more wonderful by this diversity of its islands—every shade of hue from the intense green above the near shores to the last amethyst on the horizon, which may be land or may be cloud a long day's sail away. But one thing strikes the western eye at once even more than colour, and that is the bareness of the land.

It is not the glaring bareness of limestone rocks such as makes the burning shores of Provence look half desert. The rounded slopes of Patmos and of nearly all the other islands which crowd all those lovely waters are fertile. They would bear dense growth and nourish large trees, as in antiquity they did. What has destroyed the forests has been the Mohammedan blight.

Islam is the enemy of the tree, as it is the enemy of all

patient and continuous human effort. Islam will cut down for fuel or for building or for mere devastation, but it will not be at the pains to replant, still less at the pains of protecting the young shoots against goats and other enemies. So Patmos, though it is green, is bare, like all its neighbours between Crete and the Dardanelles. We do not see, when we look on it, the things that St. John saw; we see something that has been ravaged. In St. John's time it was wooded. It even had groves of palms (a few of which remain). It was human with leaves. Now it is stripped and naked.

If that is true of the absence of trees, it is even more true of the absence of houses. There is no greater contrast between the east and the west of the Mediterranean, at any rate between the main Christian part and the shores which the Turks harried rather than governed, than this drawing back of human habitation from the sea line. There is no greater mark of what the Turk meant to the inhabitants of the Greek islands. He meant sporadic massacre and loot, both when he could not protect his subjects from piracy and when he himself fell into one of his fits of anti-Christian rage.

Men built under the shadow of that terror. They built little. They built far apart and sparsely. Their numbers declined. If we could get a full picture of what all that sea-world was in the early Christian time and compare it with what we see today we should understand what ruin false doctrine can bring upon the world. The ancient paganism, being a preparation for the Faith, did no such hurt. It was Mohammedanism, the greatest and most virulent of the heresies (and the most persistent) which must bear the blame.

Another thought which struck me as I passed those

famous but now lonely coasts was the meaning in those days—and long since—of exile. St. John was exiled to Patmos. It was conveniently near to Ephesus, and yet thoroughly cut off. It was a small place, and therefore easily guarded, yet there is here an historical problem, which I have never seen solved and which is this: what was the exact meaning of exile?

It was, we may say, a sort of free and large imprisonment. The chief burden of it (for most men) was separation from home and friends. All that we know; but how was it enforced?

The modern world is full of an elaborate and ubiquitous police system both public and private. You never know in London or Paris in any public place or vehicle, whether the person next you may not be what is prettily called "a secret agent." But that is one of the recent blessings in civilisation. Antiquity was more haphazard. A little place like Patmos could be watched fairly closely, but it could not have been impossible for an exile to make away. How did they keep an important man like Ovid marooned on the shores of the Black Sea? For the matter of that, how could Louis the Fourteenth, centuries later, be certain that a noble whom he "exiled" from his court to the provinces would stay put?

Another very much larger problem, an enormously more important question, arises in the mind as one looks at Patmos from the sea. It needs to be answered in a fashion at once delicate and profound. It is this: why did there thus arise an acute antagonism between the Catholic Church and the ancient civilisation from which we all spring? That civilisation is our own. It was the seed plot of the Faith; the Greco-Roman world was that which the Church permeated, transformed, and ultimately restored in better form after the ordeal of the Dark Ages. Why did it struggle so against the first stirrings of the Truth? The exile of St. John to Patmos was one of the very early examples of that conflict which was to endure for more than three long life-times. What was their quarrel with us? Why did Tertullian say that the twin sisters, the Empire and the Church, should be at one, *save that the Caesars could not be Christian?* Why did it take the Caesars so long to accept their destiny? We have never had a complete solution to that enigma.

We know very well why the virulent, debased, modern hostility to the Faith is what it is. It is the hatred of corruption for health, the hatred of vice for virtue. But why should that which made the height of loveliness in verse and in stone have wrestled with complete beauty, and attempted to destroy the only final harmony?

I would suggest that the battle arose from those clouded but profound intimations of the future, "the cry of the unborn," which seem in some mysterious way, to affect men before the event. They make them dimly sentient of what as yet is not, but is to be. The Catholic Church did not come to destroy but to complete. Unfortunately, that which it came to complete was too well satisfied with its own evil as well as with its own good. The threat of so much change was a mortal challenge. Hence (as it seems to me) the growing friction between the ancient Roman Empire and the Catholic Church for which that Empire was so noble a preparation. Hence I think also the explanation of the violence in which the persecutions ended. There was a sort of spasm, a life and death struggle, at the very end, which we call by the general name of the "Diocletian persecution"—though Diocletian himself, poor man, was hardly the principal culprit.

There is about the Catholic Church something absolute which demands, provokes, necessitates alliance or hostility, friendship or enmity. The truth you find unchangeable throughout the ages, and therefore it is, that on the first appearance of the Church, the challenge is already declared —and that is what is meant by Patmos.

There was very much more of course that came into my mind as I steamed slowly southward into the evening along that coast and beyond it; and of all the thoughts that crowded in this one predominated: "What a testimony it is to St. John that his high vision should have been specially challenged by the enemies of religion!" It was not only the pagan world of the Ægean coast which singled him out for an enemy. It is, and has been, much more the modern anti-Christian attack which is and has been obsessed by him.

He is well able to meet it.

Carthage

THERE IS A KIND OF RAILWAY STATION WHICH HAS NOT TO
my knowledge been written upon. Come! let me write
upon it here! It is the railway station which is hardly
worthy of being called a station at all, a wooden platform
and a wooden shed, usually upon a single line, and that
line often more of a tramway than a full-blown track.

I remember very vividly one such in Bear County, Penn-
sylvania. I shall always remember it vividly because it
was from the platform there that I saw disappearing round
the curve, through my own miscalculation, the only chance
I had of escaping from the wilds. It was not till after a
night spent in an oil-lamp shed that I could expect salvation,
promised to me for the following morning. That was forty
years ago, or not much less. No doubt there is now some
great town on the place. I seem to remember that they had
found or were finding oil, but it was so long ago that I
may be wrong.

Another such shed and platform returns to my mind
over a gulf of forty-three years. That also may have
changed, but as I saw it its title had a singular attraction
for me. There they stood, the usual appurtenances of such
halts; a wretched wooden shed, the rotting planks of a
platform—but one thing remarkable, which was a long
board set up above the platform with a name upon it, and
the name inscribed there was (in a foreign tongue) "Polar
Circle."

It was tremendous: tremendous in its humility. No hotel, no human roof of any kind, still less any triumphal arch or salute of guns, or even fireworks. I had heard of the Polar Circle all my youth, I had revered it as it should be revered—how distant, how mysterious, how great a thing! And there it was now in front of me, and no one to do it honour. No doubt in South America and in Africa one might find the opposite number to this little station or halt, and come upon a lonely weather-beaten board solemnly entitled "Equator," and probably no one to do reverence to that either. So little do men understand the gods!

But of all such wayside things, one has impressed me most. It was the simple plank which bore painted upon it, rather roughly, the single word "Carthage."

That also was very many years ago: there may be more dignity about it now. Moreover, I have passed there many times, yet it is the first impression (as usual) which remains most clear. I remember I was so moved as to get out of the little tram-train, though I had a ticket to take me further, and having got out I began to saunter up the famous hill, musing within myself. Here had lifted the towers of that imperial city, of the city that radiated over the Mediterranean and drew to itself the luxury and the wealth of every shore. "This hill," said I to myself (pressing my foot upon the roadway as though to take possession thereof), "this hill was the *Byrsa*. Not far from where I stand Scipio recited that couplet from the Iliad as he gazed upon the flames rising from the cracked walls and smelt the pungent smoke and heard the roar of his soldiery: 'There will come a day when holy Ilium itself shall perish and Priam and the people of Priam in spite of his good ashen spear.' " No one has told us from within the awful story of how Carthage fell. There was no

Josephus to record the tragedy of his own people. What we know from the conquerors is fearful enough: the women throwing themselves into the flames and their children also; the lords of the great town making of their own bodies a last sacrifice to Moloch, their god and their king.

Carthage ought not to have disappeared as it has. The victors rebuilt it. It was still the great capital. It only gradually decayed under Islam in the Middle Ages. Yet today the impression of that disappearance is so powerful that, standing on Carthage hill, one feels as though it had never re-arisen and as though the desolation were a monument to its original catastrophe.

That rise of ground is slight indeed, hardly worthy to be an Acropolis. How splendid it must have been when it was crowned by the temples of the Syrian gods and round about them the high palaces of their priests, the high palaces of their nobles, the porticos of their parliaments, the throngs of their dependent thousands.

Below me, down the slight slope, lay those twin circles which are called (wrongly I think) the ancient harbour; such small rings of water could never have held the war fleet of that sea power which was mistress of the ancient world, and which fell at last to the soldiers of the land, as sea power always falls—but not before it has had a run for its money! Hundreds of years did that aristocracy lie quite secure, because it had what we call today "command of the sea"; nor at the end could it really believe that the end had come.

Rather I fancy that Carthage must have had some great exterior harbour made of twin breakwaters to shelter some wide expanse of quiet wharfage and anchorage for the immense trade of the city. It would seem impossible that those moles have disappeared. How that should be it is difficult to understand, however powerful the sea waves, but it is more difficult to understand that there could ever have been a Carthage with no great harbour serving her. Perhaps there was an inland lake for harbour: a lagoon. As for those little circular islands, I take it they were rather the places of the port admiral's command, and that there you might have found picked galleys lying moored, head and stern, like the spokes of a wheel. But never could they have berthed the main forces of Carthage in arms, still less the crowd of her merchant shipping.

Is it not strange that the ancients hardly ever concerned themselves to portray their famous habitations? They concerned themselves with the human figure, they played continually, in stone and fresco, on the theme of their legends, but they left us no landscape. Would that we now had some such to show us how Carthage looked from the deep. We need some such thing more for Carthage than for any of her peers. We have much wherewith to rebuild Jerusalem in the mind, not a little wherewith to rebuild Athens, a great deal for the resurrection of Rome, and so with city after city of the antique world. But of Carthage nothing.

Syria

SYRIA MEANS THE COASTAL BELT OF THE EASTERN
Mediterranean. It is very hot. It is habitable and fruitful
within range of the sea-coast and of the hills behind that
coast. After that it rapidly dries up and turns into desert.
It is only a fringe.

But it has this immense importance, that men can live
there and cities can thrive there and, therefore, roads can
be established: on which account from the beginning of
recorded history armies have marched up and down Syria;
and it has afforded a perpetual battlefield.

It is odd how it has escaped damage from this perpetual
passing and repassing of armed multitudes. Some of its
cities have disappeared but most of them have survived
and its fields and vineyards have continued to be cultivated,
age after age. One corner of it and one corner alone has
become exceptionally famous, mainly through the spread
of the Christian religion. All men know of Palestine. But
Syria itself has become neither famous nor defined. It has
been but a highway. There has been a fierce patriotism
attached to Palestine, but none to Syria as a whole. No
man says proudly, "I am a Syrian"; no man mourns the loot
of Syria; no man glories in Syria's prosperity. Syria is no
one name and no one soul.

Syria was the ground of a vast historical experiment
in the story of Europe; for in Syria the West for a moment

attempted to establish itself in the East. Syria was the *venue* of that astonishing episode, the sudden business of the Crusades. The flame had been lit not there but far off in Spain, where the new Mohammedan enthusiasm had clashed at last against Christendom under the Pyrenees. Thence the battle rolled violently eastward and vast armies, which may have numbered from first to last a million men, opened a sort of debate between the orient and the occident. The effort was too much for us. We of the West at last gave way; our heavy armed knights even in their early chain armour could not stand the blast coming from the desert, the burning eastern wind. Relay after relay of western men attempted to save the beleagured fortress of Christendom, but they were at last exhausted and in the end Saladin was able to boast that he had rid Syria of "the Christian pestilence." Further efforts to bring back the occident successively failed and in our day we have seen Syria fall again into a social lethargy almost wholly oriental.

There are, indeed, the Christian communities of the sea-plain, and there has been maintained, sporadically, an effort to establish permanent troops from the West along the Syrian border. The last of these efforts has been the present English occupation of Palestine and the Jewish experiment. But such an effort cannot be final. In the long run the wind from the desert must return. It will not dry up the land; the coastal belt will always remain habitable, fertile and even luxuriant, save quite at its southern tip; but Syria which began as an oriental thing will end without a doubt as an oriental thing. There was a time indeed when it looked as though the universal culture of Greece would establish itself here against the Orient; and the great name of the young man Alexander survives everywhere to recall the ambition of the western men. But the inevitable flood of the Orient returned. It took the form of a Mohammedan enthusiasm and of the desert-men galloping through, hunched up on their short stirrups, sweeping forward on their high saddles upon the fiery little mounts of Barbary.

Is it possible that the tide will again turn, even for a moment, and that the West will re-establish itself in Syria? The thing may be doubted. It is improbable indeed. Fierce sun and burning air and that fearful wind blowing at intervals from the oven of Northern Arabia kill the opportunity and adventure of our race in such a clime.

I could wish that those who write on travel more concerned themselves with the singular effect of the air than with landscape. Many have written on Syria, but nearly all have written under the influence of its brief, its lovely, its ephemeral spring. That passed, what returns is in truth the desert.

I know what I am writing about. My own experience of men and cities has always been an experience of climate, of the air. And the air of Syria, once you have left the coast, becomes more and more the blast of a furnace from the desert. In that little strip of happier land between the dry sands and the sea great verse has flourished and, what is more important, mighty movements of doctrine: the winds of the soul have blown over it. We still call one narrow patch of it "the Holy Land." What shall we be calling it a hundred years hence or two hundred years hence?

The old struggle for Syria's battlefield has been transformed. It will revive. But in what shape we do not know.

Aleppo

THERE ARE TOWNS A DISTANT ASPECT OF WHICH IS individual, so that it strikes the memory permanently. Aleppo is of these.

If you come into it by the Antioch road, which is, I suppose, the approach most used (in Western history at least), Aleppo is first seen far off from a distant rise of land like a sort of pyramid, which is the castle hill surmounted by its magnificent stone fortress of the crusading time. There is here a sort of parallel with the aspect of Glastonbury Tor seen from far off as you come up to the Mendips from the south-west. There is the same isolated cone and marked building on the summit, though, of course, Glastonbury is on a much smaller scale. Aleppo thus proclaims itself, and its name and its portraiture make one thing in the memory. I suppose that no one in all these centuries who has come upon Aleppo thus from the west has failed to receive that unique picture in his mind.

The town spreads out round the base of the castle hill, a town too flat to interfere with the outline of that height above it; and, as always happens with elevations standing alone, that height seems far greater than it is. Whether it be artificial, like so many castle mounds, or a natural lump of rocky land added to by man, I have not the reading to say.

We may be fairly sure that the castles of Islam in Syria,

built in the crusading time, were inspired by Christian models, and this castle hill of Aleppo recalls similar and often lesser mounds in Europe: for instance, that of Norwich. But it has a feature not uncommon in Syria, more rarely seen in the West which is the clothing of the hill surface with a sheet of stone. You cannot ride up to the base of the castle wall; everywhere the earth is covered by a steep slope of dressed masonry, which no horse could manage and perhaps no man on foot either.

The other great stone fortresses of the Syrian belt were either of Christian origin, falling at last to the Mohammedans in the final failure of the Crusades, or were not gigantic, as were the French castles. They do not tower. There is nothing in Damascus, for instance, which dominates that great town as the castle of Aleppo dominates all the plain around it.

Aleppo thus fortified, and one might almost say impregnable, was one of the Ports of the Desert: the northernmost.

The meaning of these "Ports of the Desert" is this: Syria is a ribbon of land commonly fertile, watered by the streams that are nourished from the snows of Lebanon, from the springs of the limestone hills and from a rainfall decreasing as you go inland from the Mediterranean: that rainfall ceases shortly to the east of these "Ports."

Travel and trade could pass from fertile Mesopotamia to Syria along a sort of crescent, intermittently fertile, which united the watered land of the Euphrates and the Tigris with the watered land of Syria itself. But to go by way of that crescent is a long way round, and direct access from the wealth of the two rivers to the Mediterranean coast was only to be had by making straight across the barren wilderness of the Syrian desert—all baked stones

with very rare oases (such as Palmyra) in between. Therefore much of the trade and travel made right across the
desert, as the modern motor traffic makes, in a short cut;
the expense of carriage has been lessened. Thus the trade
of the further Middle East, including even that of the
distant Indies, made in a large proportion for those towns,
once larger and wealthier than they are now, which lie
along the edge of the desert all the way from Aleppo in
the north to Arabia on the south.

Aleppo may not perhaps properly be called a "Port of
the Desert," because the desert hardly comes up to its
doors; but the wilderness is near Aleppo, and Aleppo is the
first in the chain of these "ports." That chain was joined
up, as by a thread, with the South and with Egypt; this
thread was the caravan road running east of Palestine
through Moab and on to Akaba and the Red Sea. This
was that communication between the two halves of Islam
which the Crusaders never succeeded in capturing; the
"neck" which remained intact during all the furious struggle between the West and the East. Had the Crusaders
taken Damascus, they would have won their battle for
good; even if they had only permanently held Aleppo they
would have made the taking of Damascus easier. But
Aleppo, like Damascus, never fell.

There is I know not what of the Western about Aleppo.
It has always been touched by Western influence, and
today, with its big new suburbs of European houses, that
Western mark is enhanced. But Aleppo remains, like all
these Ports of the Desert, a thoroughly Eastern thing.
It will survive this last new pressure of our hopelessly
divided and perhaps declining modern Christendom.

You will look in vain among those narrow streets for
the place where Othello seized by the throat a malignant

(actually *turbaned*) Turk and smote him thus and thus. For it is but a figment of the poet's. But in any one of those tortuous alleys it might have happened—and it might happen to-day. For Aleppo keeps up a fine hatred for the unbeliever.

Aleppo is thoroughly Oriental also in this: that the poets of Islam have made a fantastic mirage of it, and particularly of its river—so called.

The rivers of Damascus are indeed rivers of Damascus: glorious great rushing streams of mountain water, as fresh and vigorous as any in the Alps. But the river of Aleppo is (if I may say so without too much offending the guardian spirits of the place) a narrow, dirty ditch, stagnant, foul with refuse: almost a drain; and there is very little of it at that. Were the West to remain master of Aleppo for another lifetime or so, I think it would be covered up as the men of Athens now propose to cover up the thrice-famous Ilyssus, and as Londoners covered up the Fleet and Paris the Bièvre.

But the West will hardly remain in Aleppo long. I fancy if I were to go back to Aleppo from the higher places a generation hence I should still see the River of Aleppo playing its degraded part. Yet the poets of Islam talked of it as though it were one of the streams of Paradise!

And so goodbye, Aleppo. I doubt if you will ever see me again: but that will not make you mourn, for you are too old. Your name was already famous 3,000 years ago.

The Bekaa

THERE LIES IN THE NEAR EAST A PIECE OF LANDSCAPE SO
astonishing that I wonder it has not taken a great place in
literature. It lies immediately behind the Lebanon mountains, and the people of that country call it "The Bekaa."
I do not know whether I have the spelling right or not,
nor indeed is there a right spelling for any Arabic word.
The transliteration of Arabic into European alphabets has
become so much a matter of different schools and different
tastes that an unlearned man like myself has no choice but
to copy the example before his eyes, so I have called this
place "The Bekaa" because I see it spelt thus in the book
on Syria which I bought for my travel.

Anyhow, the word means "the depression," and a
memorable depression it is! No man who has seen it will
ever forget it. It will stand out in the mind of anyone, however widely travelled, as one of the marvels of this world.
It stands out in my mind with the Araxas valley in the
Pyrenees, with the Black Canyon and not half a dozen
other things of the kind.

The Lebanon is a long, strikingly simple steep and very
high ridge running from north to south along the sea
coast of the eastern Mediterranean, and so close to the
waters that the plain between them and the fistric of land
is but a strip. There are no intervening confusions of
tumbled land; nothing of what are called in America foot-

hills. The great keen ridge lifts straight up into Heaven like a gigantic "hog's-back," to quote the Surrey name, and as one climbs it by the main road to Damascus from Beyrout one wonders what there can be beyond. On the analogy of many such keen cut lines of height one might think the Lebanon here to be an escarpment, and for my part, when I first went up from the sea into these mountains, I thought I should find upon the far side of them a plateau, probably desertic and gradually sinking towards Damascus and the desert level.

What I did see when I had crossed the summit was something quite other! There opened abruptly below me a counter slope as steep and nearly as profound as that by which I had risen from the sea plain. It fell away at once into the depths, and beyond those depths another ridge, apparently as high as Lebanon and facing Lebanon, the anti-Lebanon, rose up abruptly and barred all view to the East. Thus between Lebanon and anti-Lebanon, walled in on either side, cut off from the world, was this very deep and silent valley. It seemed to be a countryside to itself, clearly defined from the beginning of the world and apart from all things to the one side or the other. And anyone coming upon it as I did might say to himself, as did I also, "Here is a Kingdom! Here is a world of its own whereunto men reach only rarely and with difficulty. Its immense mountain walls defend it absolutely, and between them there is fertility, wealth and peace."

So it should be, for this extraordinary valley, "The Bekaa," is as much one thing, separate from all its neighbours as is the Alsatian Plain. And its climate is such that one might expect it to be filled with gardens surrounding separate cities of men: woods also and great stretches of green pasture. The heat of the desert is fended off from it. The sea winds when they blow are fended off also.

The snows of Lebanon and of anti-Lebanon and of mighty Hermon which stands guardian at the end of that valley to the south feed the depression with perennial streams. These unite to form along the northern half of it the Orontes, along the south of it the Litany, while under the shoulder of Hermon itself still further southward are the sources of the Jordan and the little lakes above the Sea of Galilee.

Time was when the valley of the Orontes, the upper valley in this same depression, and the converse valley of the Litany were drained and tamed and subject to man's use. They had their farms on either bank and their grazing fields, their plantations, and their copses. There was provision for a great multitude of men and their flocks in "The Bekaa," and apparently from the beginning it had been a safe and choice habitation for men. Its wealth also nourished great cities of which the mistress was Baalbek, the Town of the Sun. Here lived in the beginning some titanic race, or at least one that worked titanic things. The city walls and the foundations of the City Temples were built of huge stones the size of houses and brought hither heaven knows how. Such inhuman masonry was designed to stand fast forever. No battering ram, you might say, could shift such rocks as these. Fire could never touch them. The city which had stood from some immemorial beginning would stand on for centuries and centuries more. Men had known it 4,000 years ago. They would continue to know it to the end of time.

It has proved otherwise. "Baalbek" itself was mortal, and even those cyclopean stones which are like the rocks of nature rather than the handiwork of man have been scattered.

The fertile land with its wealth of springs and waters bears fruit no more. It has run to swamp. It is not summoned to support mankind nor does it support it. A group of missionaries did what they could some time ago to reclaim this abandoned natural wealth, but they have had little effect upon "The Bekaa." It is as though the genius of the place after his centuries upon centuries of civic magnificence had fallen into a lethargy and slept. It is as though a paralysis had fallen upon all human energy along those streams.

I could fancy that someone would have made upon "The Bekaa" a legend of some curse fallen through neglect of the gods. But there is no such legend that I heard nor even a memory among the village wanderers therein of the time when the great town and the great temple under the protection of the sun god gloried in its treasure, and sent those of its blood to rule in Rome itself.

"The Bekaa" remembers none of these things. It seems to think itself now a swamp abandoned from the beginning of the world and certainly has no hope of a resurrection nor desire for one. If such a thing should come it must come from without. In the place itself hope and energy died long ago.

Yet from what cause? There was no drying up of fountains. There was no desolation of sand-storms. There was not even the passage of great armies, for these went up and down westerly up the coast, or easterly beyond the mountains. "The Bekaa" supported no international road. It seems to have held no great traffic from Antioch to the north or Jerusalem to the south, or to have exchanged its crops and timber with the rich ports to the west. It was not apparently destroyed from without, nor ravaged nor looted, nor rendered barren by some caprice of water level or the choking up of its springs. It simply died of fatigue, as it were, and promises so to remain dead, unalterably for generations, with only the huge ruins to testify to what it was.

Pursue that only road eastward, finely engineered through the marsh, come to the opposing wall of anti-Lebanon, climb through this to a half-concealed col, and there lies before you, like a sea, the desert, and at your feet the fertility of Damascus standing in its orchards and gardens fed by the gushing waters of anti-Lebanon.

That is alive enough! Damascus never dies. But those other proud cities that were the contemporaries of its youth are gone, and the inner valley is silent.

Antioch

I KNOW NOT HOW IT MAY BE WITH OTHERS, BUT I CANNOT even approach the name of Antioch—let alone my memories of the city, of the dwindled but still sacred city—without a feeling of awe.

If Antioch were still a great centre which men would visit and make familiar with a number of modern memories I should not feel this so much; indeed, the place would have been written about so often that one more allusion to it would seem not worth while. If it were one of those places from which life has disappeared, one of those famous ruins which men venerate as they might a shrine, and are the more able to venerate because there is no modern life to disturb them, then again it would have been written and over-written.

But it so happens that Antioch is neither the one nor the other. It is still a living town, indeed delightfully alive, but so much smaller than the huge original capital of Syria, the imperial city of the East for more than 1,000 years, that the name seems to attach to a thing completely changed. It is as though centuries hence one could come across a place still called "London," and find that you could walk out from the centre to fields in a quarter of an hour.

Yet here it was, in this now little place (and charming), that things of such tremendous import to our civilisation and its creative religion took place. Antioch was the true second capital of the growing Church. It was in a way more productive of the future than Jerusalem itself. It became the centre to which not only those who had fled from Jerusalem converged, but to which men came from all sides who desired immediately after the Resurrection to meet with or to be adopted into the new strange vivid body which here in Antioch for the first time took the name of Christian. Here was St. Peter Bishop by all tradition, the second intermediary see between Jerusalem and Rome. Here the missionaries were deputed and authorised to go forth upon their journeys. For it was here, not at Jerusalem, nor at Damascus nor in his own native Cilicia, that St. Paul had authority from the Church to go out and preach, taking with him another equally authorised companion. Here you may still see the grotto in which St. Peter celebrated the Eucharist, and here it seemed for a moment as though the central point of the new Christian life would reside.

It is remembering such things as these that the eye strains to catch the first sight of Antioch as the traveller comes down from across the high mountain ridge of Amanus to the North of the city. The ancient harbour of Antioch, at the mouth of its river, a day's march down from the city, has long silted up and disappeared. We enter now from Alexandretta, and between us and Antioch itself lies that long, high mountain, still guarded by the ruins of the first crusading castle commanding the road. The road has been rebuilt by the French, broad and with a fine surface; the gradients are easy, and the motor takes you from the harbour over the height and down towards the valley and plain of the Orontes as it might in the best developed districts of Europe. Yet off the road on either side conditions are what they have been since the breakdown of our civilisation in the East on the defeat of the Crusaders 700 years ago. The Turk has ruined everything. And Europe, now come back again precariously, must attempt to reconstruct—if indeed it be given time.

The road sinks rapidly down by curves on the mountain side to the flat below, where a very large but shallow mere, miles long and broad, has been allowed to spread undyked since the retreat of our Western civilisation from this place. The Orontes does not flow through this mere, but just beyond, and as one goes near it the fields grow green, orchards and trees appear—most characteristic among them the lovely spires of the cypress—and mingled with these trees very far off are the centre towers and the low roofs of the little town. And he who comes upon it thus, so restricted and gathered upon itself along the riverside, asks himself, "Can this be Antioch? Can this be the city, the name of which filled the earlier world and had magic for all men for century upon century, from its first founding by a chief general of Alexander to the last Mohammedan conquest when the crusading effort failed?"

Behind it, against the midday sun, rises a high, abrupt, arresting wall of dark precipitous mountain-land looking over the flat of the Valley of the Orontes river to the great mere beyond, to the opposing wall of Amanus. That high dark ridge to the South against the sun is serrated at its extreme summit, by what one takes at first to be rocks of a fantastic shape, but on looking more narrowly one finds them to be not rocks but the bastions of the city wall, and the sight of such a defence more than 1,000 feet above one, towering into the air and already become a part, as it were, of the earth, suddenly illuminates the mind with a vision of what Antioch once was. These enormous walls, with a circuit of miles and miles, climbing and mastering the mountain side, give one the limits of the imperial capital, and then one sees the majesty that was Antioch.

Where now are the gardens and the orchards and the one or two small vineyards of the city and beyond them again waste land with here and there ploughland upon the open fields: all over those miles once stood the palaces and temples of the Seleucidae. The great colonnade ran there from East to West, nearly following the river bank, and on an island of the river itself stood the royal house whence orders had gone out against the Maccabees and for the resistance to Persian invasion, and for the attempt to check the advancing tide of the Roman armies. There, while Antioch was still in its splendour, Ignatius commanded the Church and testified to its nature and the authority of Bishops, to the unity of the Catholic body, in a fashion which the worst enemies of the Faith have never been able to get over. I have met only one man in my life who pretended to be rid of that evidence, and to neglect the testimony of St. Ignatius, and he did it by the simple circular process of saying that the letters were impossible because in the time of St. Ignatius they could not have been written.

The ghost of old Antioch lies there, within those miles and miles of walls crowning the mountains, and from it in a vision one may see the Church, now founded at last, spreading outwards throughout the world, and under its title one reads the names of Paul, of Barnabas, of Luke, and Peter, of Mark, of Ignatius. But with a shock of returning reality one finds no such thing as the vast concourse of men and buildings which made famous, so famous, a name.

One finds a delightful little town wherein men of every sort, the Mohammedan, the Eastern Christian in schism, the Eastern Christian in union with Rome, the small congregation of the Latin rite, with a church wherein a Westerner may follow Mass as you would at home.

One finds also a hotel, domestic, clean, well managed, with the wine and the cooking of France; and one finds, without the stress or (what is worse) the vulgarity of towns much visited, all that is needed for the modern kind of travel.

Antioch in all this stands unique among the places of Syria. Long may it so remain, and I believe it will. For it is not yet on the road to anywhere, and even though Alexandretta be developed (as it probably will be if the French retain their hold upon all this), the railway will tunnel under the Amanus and I doubt whether very many will get off at Antioch before reaching the port. The Orontes Valley may be developed again, but it will take time, and the fruitful land upstream will bear wealth as it did of old, until perhaps all down the profound central valley above Baalbek to the Litany, and Hermon and the source of the Jordan itself, our civilisation shall build up again what it built up and maintained all those generations ago. Perhaps the ruin and destruction wrought by Islam will be undone. But even if that happens Antioch will, please God, remain on one side of the main way, isolated and happy. It has done its work; it has retired; and its old age is excellent.

So of all the towns that belonged to the past, and yet are not dead, nor even dying, Antioch will remain most fixedly with me, I think. It bears so great a name, that name calls up so vast a fame, it is the inheritor of so many centuries,

that it is dominant. Nor, though Antioch is decayed, can
one contemplate it as one can the dead Cities of the Desert.
One cannot indulge in Antioch a meditation upon the
mortality of things, for it lives, and lives strongly enough.
It is not, as the phrase goes, "A shadow of its former self."
It is rather a lesser substitute of its former self—a much
lesser substitute, but a still vigorous thing. Everywhere in
its few streets and even over the great area of deserted
land to the East, which once was covered by the city,
up to the crest of the mountains, where the line of the
wall still shows against the sky, one feels a latent life. If
a port were arranged for Antioch, it would probably rise
again, if not to its old magnificence, yet to something
fairly great.

One feels about Antioch that if it were to extend again
over its now empty lanes, to reach its ancient limits, and
to rebuild the full circuit of its walls, it would not be a
resurrection, but a natural return. It is as though a man
had gone on a long journey and left his household on
board wages, and shut up three-quarters of the rooms,
and left but a little income for general upkeep, but might
be expected to come home.

There is no town on which I feel more curious as to its
future. Of many old towns that are really dead, one may be
sure they will never be towns again. That is true, for instance, of the mere vestige of Aquilea, the Mother of
Venice. You would not know, had you not first been told,
that a town had stood there at all, and so it is with the
Hippo of St. Augustine in Africa. With Antioch it is not
so. You feel as you walk about its still lively alleys and
small square places that the sap still stirs.

For one thing, there is the liveliness of the river. Wherever water is alive, the noise of it gives life to all things

around it; and the great wheel on the river at Antioch adds to the activity of the stream. That stream, the Orontes, has a strange little history of its own. Starting between the Lebanon and anti-Lebanon in the now neglected inner valley whereof so much has gone back to marsh, and wherein such great works of men have disappeared, the Orontes flows northwards, narrow and not deep, with few to watch it, few farms for it to nourish. It remains so narrow a thing on to where it bends westwards and makes for the sea. It is only just more considerable than its twin—the Litany—which also rises in that deep hidden valley, but flows southwards, reaching the sea, as the Orontes does, by a turn round the end of the mountains.

No: is the little life of the small Orontes the only quickening thing about Antioch. There is also the interchange of the religions, and their worshippers, and some moderate measure of travel, men coming from Alexandretta southwards, or from Aleppo eastward to the junction of Antioch. There is an active body of scholars working through excavation at the rediscovery of the old town, and everywhere there is enough of the past for the traveller to see that past at work in his mind. The citizens of Antioch in her great centuries from just after Alexander to the failure of the Crusades—that is, for very much more than a thousand years—would be shocked indeed to see the very shrunken city of today. They would find nothing of their own there. The Colonnades were long ago cast down, and every majesty of building has disappeared. But we who so often find on a famous site nothing but dereliction and silence, can take some sustenance from Antioch, and build in fancy upon what remains.

"Here," said I to myself, "stood that Tower which the Normans entered. Here was that bridge (I believe the present bridge is on the same site) over which the knights rode out to that very critical battle in which the Mohammedans nearly recovered the city. Here in the fields to the east stood that theatre wherein thousands upon thousands of the citizens and slaves were absorbed upon a show when the Persian host came bursting in."

If any traveller should have the patience, which I had not, to climb the very steep high crest to the south, and follow along the walls, so startlingly surviving mile upon mile, he will not only, in looking down on the void below and the now uninhabited places, be filled with the magnitude of what Antioch was, but will also be in something like communion with it. Because on that one line, standing as those walls do, upon a ridge defended by the steepness of the approach from the north, these ramparts bridge the distance between the time of their building and our own.

But the monument of the great past which most remains with the traveller is that place wherein tradition has it St. Peter celebrated the Eucharist. I have called it "a monument," but I use the word only in the sense of a still standing witness of the past; for as it now is, the thing is no more than a cave. Such was it, presumably, when first it was put to Christian use nearly 1900 years ago. It is more foolish to deny tradition in things of this sort than to fall into the opposite vice of credulity. For my part, I cannot believe that an origin so famous in a community destined to such expansion would ever have been forgotten.

That cave is now quite isolated on the further boundaries of the city, and it was in such outer parts of the great towns that the early Christian communities would gather. Perhaps there was a group of habitations above the mountain stream, which here runs down to the Orontes, through what was once the edge of a densely peopled city, and past those scenes, a record of which, intimately associating Antioch in our minds, was made by the early Church. Nothing has come in modern times to vulgarise or to over-lay this memorable site. The cave remains lonely, as it has been, presumably, for many hundreds of years, for though the Antioch of the Crusaders was still a great town, it had already shrunk within its ancient boundaries.

Antioch has no centre, as has each one of the remaining towns associated with the beginnings of our religion. There is nothing in it like the Church of the Sepulchre in Jerusalem, or the great basilica—now Mosque—in Damascus. If there be a kernel to the place it is this still remote and half-deserted cave: first stage on the road from Pentecost to the human torches of Nero and to the crosses on the Vatican hill.

Damascus

I WROTE A LITTLE TIME AGO ON ALEPPO. I THEN ALLUDED
to Damascus. Let me return to-day to Damascus, for it is
of permanent interest.

The town has already stood there for 4,000 years and is
still what it has always been, the key of the Syrian belt.
This "Syrian belt" is the bridge beween Asia and the
wealth of the African coast, north of the Sahara Desert.
It is essentially the link between Asia and the age-long ac-
cumulated wealth of the Nile. Caravans for untold centuries have crossed the desert between Mesopotamia and the
Syrian belt and to-day mechanised transport crosses it. But
it remains a formidable obstacle in human intercourse and
probably will always so remain. There is sufficient rainfall
for crops and animals and men along the Mediterranean
shore of the Levant and upon the mountains immediately
inland: notably the great parallel ridges of the Lebanon.
And this rainfall is stored naturally by the limestone formation of those hills, which is continued southward in Moab
and in Palestine. That formation is a sort of natural cistern
or reservoir, while on Lebanon itself the snows melting in
the spring continue to furnish nourishment. But when you
get to the east of this fertile strip, which is in places only a
long day's ride across, you are in the desert.

Damascus stands on the desert side of the anti-Lebanon,

that is, of the high mountain clot in the middle of the Syrian belt, about half way between North and South. It is nourished by a magnificent water supply of mountain torrents rushing down from the snows of the great hills above. In less than a long day's walk those waters are swallowed up by the burning sand, first in a sort of marsh and afterwards disappearing altogether; but at Damascus itself, right at the foot of the great hills, they are still abundant and clear: a sort of miracle in the eyes of the nomad desert men, their camels and their horses, for whom Damascus has been from, I suppose, the beginning of human affairs, the goal of all transport across the burnt intervening land. So it was in Abraham's time, so it is to-day. Damascus is therefore a symbol. One might call it a bunch of symbols. It is a symbol of the permanent physical conditions that run throughout history; the permanent geographical limits of human settlement, government and war.

It is a type or symbol also of another thing permanent in human affairs and present even to-day when armament has so greatly changed—I mean the struggle for the key point. Damascus is the key of the Syrian belt. Who holds Damascus holds all that narrow fertile strip from Antioch southward to the half desert gap which is the gate of Egypt, the Sinaitic coast-line which the road from Palestine to Egypt always followed and which the railway follows to-day.

We are tired in this generation of ours, with its perpetual alarms and intolerable war-menace, of such words as "key point." It is enough to say that this or that place is a "key point" to put off the modern reader; for the phrase is used nearly always without explanation and most of the time without reason. Nevertheless, when it is used rationally, it is a most valuable phrase, explaining the past and contemporary things. Damascus is the key of maritime Syria and of all that famous land which held and holds Antioch itself, Tyre, Sidon, the shrines of Adonis, Baälbek, the Cedars of Lebanon, Mount Hermon, the Holy Land, Moab; and Damascus is the key of all that for two reasons: because it cuts the alternative road from North to South and because it is central.

Every government that has been seated in Damascus—first the Assyrian, then the Greek, then the Roman, then the early Caliphs—could and did send out and receive orders from the North and from the South of the Syrian belt and from the coast thereof by the shortest lines. The same government holding Damascus, and having garrisons on the sea coast close at hand, can prevent all movement of armies and even of land commerce on any great scale between Egypt and Asia.

And Damascus has one last symbolic character. It is the test of Islam's success or failure.

When the fierce Mohammedan enthusiasm first suddenly arose, almost exactly thirteen centuries ago, it was the capture of Damascus at the outset that founded Islamic power. Thenceforward the East had returned, and the Grecian culture and all that is meant by Europe and our civilisation had been pushed back Westward. Today Damascus is still symbolic of that come and go. Islam is there under tutelage, but the Western hold on it is precarious. The town is still wholly Oriental, and bids fair so to remain.

If you had come into Damascus when Pompey was in command there, before the final conquest of Jerusalem, you would have seen a Western city, the colonnades, the architecture, all the externals of a Graeco-Roman thing. Such it was when St Paul lay there blinded. Such it still was when the early Church gathered not within its walls but at Antioch. So it had been for more than two centuries, a Greek thing; so it was to remain for nearly seven centuries more. But had you come into Damascus in the days of Charlemagne, 800 years after Pompey, and more than 1,000 after Alexander, you would have found it already in the main Oriental, and thenceforward more and more did it lose our inheritance and take on the strange new aspect which we everywhere associate with Islam now. The Great Church of St John (a Roman basilica, I suppose?) is now a mosque. The spirit of the whole place has been transformed in those centuries from the one thing to the other, from the Occident to the Orient. And only when, if ever, Damascus is retransformed again to be a Western thing, shall we know that the tide has turned; nor perhaps will this ever happen.

This ebb and flow in the great human ocean, this surge of our race Eastward and the return of the current back Westward after generations and centuries, is a movement of which we moderns are little aware, but it determines history. We are perhaps today at this very moment, the mid-twentieth century, about to see another change: either the resurrection of Islam, the reaffirmation of its power and a further assault from the East against the West, or what is less likely (because we Europeans have lost our unity), a return of the West Eastward and a European stamp set again upon the whole of the Mediterranean and its shores, even to Mesopotamia.

Damascus is then, after Rome, the most famous town in the world. It is famous throughout the Mohammedan world as the original place whence the first Mohammedan Emperors governed and where their great hero Saladin is buried and for a hundred other reasons. It is famous throughout the Christian world through the action of the Church which has spread all over the West the knowledge of the Gospels; and of the Old Testament and of the Acts of the Apostles.

Many an ignorant man in the wilds of some distant European colony, who has but a vague idea of Rome itself, has a vivid picture in his mind of Damascus and could tell you all the story of St Paul and his escape over the wall of the city. And right away in the depths of Asia some Mohammedan tribesman from the hills who has only vaguely heard of Rome, if that, will know the name of Damascus.

Now when you come to Damascus for the first time, even if you come to it the right way (which is from over the mountains), you may be surprised to see how little its outward appearance seems to justify so great a fame. You do not see a cluster of domes and minarets, such as you see from far off on the approach to Cairo, or from the water as you come in to Constantinople. There is not even some point of view from which a picture of the city can be universally recognised.

All the world is familiar with certain typical aspects of Paris and London and Rome and the rest, and on seeing a photograph people recognise the place at once though they have never been there; but there is nothing of the sort to be done with Damascus. It is just a mass of houses with flat roofs in the ordinary Oriental fashion, a few squat domes and not a single feature which the eye can fix upon as characteristic. It has one very famous building which used to be the Church of St. John the Baptist, and is called his burial place, and which is now a mosque, but there is nothing particular about it; it is just one large transformed Roman hall.

There is one exceedingly famous corner, the tomb of Saladin, but it is a tiny place, the more impressive when you get there for its small size but in no way outstanding. There are large and famous covered markets as you find in all Oriental towns, but with commonplace ugly arched corrugated-iron roofs. In general, there are a hundred towns less famous and more distinguished: for you may fairly say of Damascus that it is not outwardly distinguished at all.

And yet as a bit of history it is amazing! It has stood there under the same name for a great deal more than four thousand years. You already find it in the Egyptian inscription of four thousand years ago and it is spoken of as though it were then already a place of immemorial establishment.

Now why is all this? Why was Damascus during all those generations of men the chief place of Syria: the central point about which all the story of Syria seems to turn? It is not the centre of any fruitful piece of land, it is not a seaport, it is difficult to get at, the earth is sterile on every side about it, and the desert begins almost at its gates.

Yet the possession of Damascus has always decided the possession of the Near East as a whole. Whoever remains master of Damascus is master of all the country between Asia Minor and Egypt. As long as Greece and as long as Rome held Damascus the Near East was Greek and Roman. When the Mohammedans took it thirteen hundred years ago, all the Near East turned Mohammedan at once, politically, and gradually became Mohammedan in religion. If the Crusaders had taken it in their first campaign just before the year 1100, the Crusades would have been a success instead of a failure, and even if they had succeeded in taking it on their second attempt half a century later the Near East might have been conquered back from Mohammedanism and might be Christian today. The third Crusade by which we lost the Holy Land had Damascus for its Mohammedan base and it was through the streets of Damascus that the relic of the True Cross was dragged at the tail of a horse after the Mohammedans had taken Jerusalem.

If tomorrow Damascus is lost, which is possible enough, all the Near East, including Egypt, will soon after be lost to European Control.

At Damascus all the great highroads meet and on Damascus all the approaches and departures converge.

At first sight, I say, no one could recognise that. All is desert to the east of it, to the west is a high wild range of mountains without even a village upon them. Beyond those mountains, as you go towards the sea, there is a profound desolate valley thousands of feet deep and quite narrow; beyond that valley again another high and deserted range of mountains, the Lebanon. Only when you have crossed the Lebanon do you see at your feet, half a day's march away, the shores of the Mediterranean, which is the universal highway of all our ancient civilisation.

But Damascus is more important than any harbour on the Mediterranean because an order given from Damascus, or news conveyed to Damascus, from any point between the Tigris and Euphrates and the Mediterranean can be conveyed or issued more quickly than from any other point. The caravans crossing the desert from Mesopotamia found the market of Damascus at the end of their journey. A rider with despatches going north to Antioch or south towards Egypt was, in Damascus, at the very middle of the whole affair. The string of towns that lie along the edges of the desert and that were once more populous than they

now are (many have even decayed and disappeared) were
joined up by the main North-South road which ran under
the mountains all the way from Asia Minor to Arabia; and
from Damascus one determined ride westwards across the
mountains could cut all the communications along the sea
coast.

The importance of Beyrouth lies in the fact that it is
the nearest seaport to Damascus. Nazareth was the halting
place of the caravans going down to the southern half of
the sea coast from Damascus. Aleppo, Homs and Hama
lived as they did because they were on the Damascus road,
and whoever garrisons Damascus can cut the line of transport which is the backbone of Syria.

That is why Damascus always has been and presumably
always will be the critical town upon the fate of which
the fate of Syria depends.

It became by a rather slow process the most intensely
Mohammedan of the Syrian towns, and by this time it is
the place from which the resurrection of Mohammedanism, if it is to come, will start. If the Europeans lose Damascus they will lose Jerusalem as a matter of course, and
the artificial division between the English and the French
"mandates" will disappear.

I sometimes think that if one were to re-visit the town
sufficiently often the spirit of it would grow upon one in
spite of its lack of distinction. I hope indeed I shall return
and perhaps under less easy circumstances than those of
today (and even today things are somewhat perilous there).
The broad fresh torrents rushing in their stone channels
through the town (soon to be lost in the sands to the east),
the distant verdure of the garden belt between the houses
and the desert, the mountains towering to the east in a wall

above one, all these rather than the city itself are what remain as a picture in the mind. There is through its immense age, through the enormous part it has played and through its invincible capacity of resistance, something which I am sure would grow upon one even in the mere streets of the city.

Yet for my part the spiritual centre of it for me is the tomb of Saladin. I was almost tempted to pray there as one might at the tomb of Charlemagne. Saladin was abominably treacherous and cruel, and the romantic legend made up about him by the enemies of Christendom, heretical and other, is moonshine; but he was a very great soldier and that is something never to be despised.

Nazareth

A STRANGER OF THE WEST COMING INTO THE HOLY LAND
does well to enter by the North, and to approach either by
the Damascus road or the coast.

That is the way much the most of those who have found
out this singular small piece of the world, with its enormous
fortunes, have travelled. So came in the merchants from beyond the desert from the beginning of time, the caravans of
Asia, the bales from India and Persia. They made either up
the Euphrates to where it passes near habitable land, where
Aleppo now is, and so down south along the edge of the
mountains till they reached Damascus; or else straight across
the waste from rare well to well until they struck Damascus
directly from the east, the first habitation of men for many
·days.

The Crusaders came down by the coast between Lebanon and the sea. But from the south was no general approach to Palestine, save by conquerors, and therefore he
who would enter by the common door had best use the
north.

Coming thus, the gate of the country is Nazareth. But
one who is considering the unique significance of Palestine,
the episode of these few years—half a young lifetime—
which count indefinitely more than all that went before
them—Nazareth is the true beginning of his journey for a

reason more profound than geography and history: Nazareth is the Home.

Bethlehem is the actual birthplace, but Bethlehem is part of the Tragedy. In situation as in the character of its events it counts with the Holy Places of the Passion. It is adjacent to Jerusalem and therefore to Calvary and the Tomb. It is associated with Herod's massacre and with the Flight of the Holy Family. The Birth stands hard by the Death and Sacrifice, a symbol of what most men find, that they end where they began.

But Nazareth was that place in which all the years in which a man is made were passed, from the first memories, through boyhood to maturity. Nazareth is the habitation, and the mother's house. To those of a full religion, Nazareth is especially filled with the silence of Our Lady and her presence.

It is in tune with all this: a happy, shining little town, climbing upwards, in a fold of high but gentle hills, the centre of those Galilean highlands which look so pure and cool from the half desert below and beyond Jordan. For, as the Damascus road plunges rapidly down out of the steppe into the narrow, over-heated trench of the river above the lake, the green heights of Galilee above and beyond are a small separate country deserving a name of its own: something much better than the arid wastes that follow in barren waves of stone southward into Judea: something more human and more blessed than the stifling gorge to the west, where the Jordan runs deeper and deeper, with an increasing fever of heat to the abomination of the Dead Sea: something more private than the rich flat of Esdraelon, the broad sea plain to the west.

These Galilean hills have been called a watch tower, as indeed the separate height of Tabor, of the Transfiguration, on the south of them is, for it commands the whole land; and from it the Mediterranean, a long day's march away below, seems close at hand. They might be called also a citadel, but a citadel of peace; and Nazareth is their heart.

How much fresher it is than the other little towns of that worn land, and, as it were, younger! I would add: "How more Christian!" The convents and monasteries have taken possession of it as they have not any other town—and the soul of it is the shrine of the Annunciation. There is in that Sacred Place no continuous antiquity as there is elsewhere. The church is of the last few generations, and in a style neither recent enough to be taken for granted nor old enough to be venerable.

The great church which Constantine built has long ago suffered the attack of our repeated enemies and fallen to ruin; only the stumps of its columns, some few, remain: here and there fragments of its mosaic floor. The existing church is built upon a fraction of the old site and on a different axis. But the air of authenticity remains. It is the very spot. And if anyone ridicule such a sense of certitude and call it an illusion or a phantasy, let him take the matter more prosaically and ask himself what, after all, would be probable, and whether the vulgar scepticism of the nineteenth century was not much more irrational and whether those who still follow it are not suffering from a belated superstition? It is a point to which I shall return when I come to the Holy Sepulchre, but I will introduce it here at the outset of the journey, for it affects every site connected with the Predication and Passion of Our Lord.

I repeat—what, after all, would be probable? Eliminate all that the sceptic does not admit to be true. Grant him, for the sake of this argument, that the early Church was a pack of enthusiasts suffering from the wildest illusions; even so, would its members not retain a fixed knowledge of what were, to them, the most important places in all the world, and of all time? A man may be laughed at for affirming that Kenilworth Castle is haunted, but there is no doubt that Kenilworth Castle is there. *That* is not an illusion and he must know it before he thinks it haunted.

It is historically certain that the Christian community had a continuous existence in Palestine for the better part of a lifetime after the Crucifixion and Resurrection of Our Lord. When the final Roman attack on Judea came, there had been all those years in which to familiarise its members with the places associated with Our Lord's life. Is it conceivable that the home of His childhood and the house which His Mother best remembered would have been forgotten?

It was a time of constant coming and going, especially in that particular land. Nazareth was on the caravan road from Damascus to the sea and on the main road which ran northward from Jerusalem. The time was a time of high civilisation and of detailed record. Is it conceivable that the men of the first century, enemies as well as friends, would have neglected and forgotten the Home whence this New Thing—so detested by the official Jewish world and the mass of the Jewish people, so cherished as the salvation of the world by those who were to found the Church—proceeded?

It is not conceivable to a man with any knowledge of how men's minds work or with a competent use of his reason that the site of Our Lady's Annunciation would be forgotten; and if it seemed conceivable to the nineteenth century sceptic it was because he had lost his commonsense.

He prided himself on his rationalism, yet all he so firmly believed was a mere mass of affirmation flying in the face of human experience and of the most obvious rules of history.

No; those who have lost the Faith may deny the Annunciation, for mysteries are not demonstrable, but that part of earth which witnessed the Annunciation is certain enough; more certain than most of the sites that are pointed out as matters of course in Profane History. A man may worship there in security; he is in the very place.

I said at the beginning of this that Nazareth was, for various reasons, the right entry into the Holy Land: the main gate. There is a last reason which should be remembered and it is perhaps the best.

Nazareth is Joy. We begin the Rosary with the commemoration of joy—we only go on later to the suffering. It is the process of human life, for the beginnings of it are happy and its tragedy is made by the passing of time. So in the greatest of human lives, which was also divine, Joy came first and the Agony at the end—before the Glory, which last does not belong to this world. You will find human joy at Nazareth, the blessed seclusion of childhood and the as yet unwounded years.

Nazareth was also the scene of the first tribulations and the first opposition; but the note of the place and its meaning lie in the Holy Childhood, and the earlier maturity when all that should come was still unknown to the world. Now in travel a man finds this about Nazareth: that such a note endures to this day.

Capharnaum

He makes but a false picture of those supreme three years during which the Godhead created the Catholic Church, if he imagine them to have been passed amid a pastoral and simple people of the mere debased oriental sort, such as we find for the most part in that desolate countryside today.

The scene of the Gospels and, in particular this Lake of Tiberias, which was the nucleus of all that went before the Passion, the stage on which or from which doctrine and revelation were proclaimed, was, in Our Lord's day, a scene of greatness, wealth and splendour; of high civilisation and of man by his creative power adding all that he could add to nature.

Where there were so many rich there were many, many more of the poor; but the world in which Our Lord and His Apostles moved, the surroundings of all that story— of the teaching from the boat, of the Transfiguration, of the Sermon on the Mount, of the casting out of devils and of that turning point, the confession of St. Peter—was a world which, to the eye and to the ear and to all the senses of those who passed through its thronged porticoes, was a high and exalted world, comparable to, but far more dignified than, the wealthy centres of today in our teeming western Europe.

Its civilisation was Greek. That civilisation was superimposed upon an older population, mainly Jewish in faith (though largely also Pagan), Semitic in tongue but in dress presumably and in general habit much what the rest of the Mediterranean people were. The dress was *not* what the Arab dress is today: *not* the modern Oriental garments in which it is still fashionable to represent Our Lord and His Apostles.

Stand on the high land to the north and east of the little shore plain of Genezareth, and look down those few miles of water, eight miles across at their broadest stretch. You see the lake narrowing down to the southward, the high hills closing round about it, forbidding to the left and to the right; at the extreme end of your view the lump of land on which lay Gadara, and the opening of that oppressive trench, deep dug below the level of the Mediterranean, the Jordan valley. Here and there you see a few new houses springing up, much more rarely the ruins, often but a stone or two, of something older; empty wastes of reed on the flat shores and some way off on the western bank, the only agglomeration which seems worthy of a name, rather a large ramshackle village than a city, still called in its degradation Tiberias, and still overhung by the dark rock on which was planted its citadel. For the rest, nothing. You are fortunate if you so much as see one sail on that flat, shining oval of water.

But in those old days it was a pageant. All round the shores of that inland water was a succession of fine towns, in an almost uninterrupted ring, passing one into the other as do those pleasure-places which we build today along the shores of the Channel; but how much more glorious!

Capharnaum was a great place, there to your right; where even now for three-quarters of a mile or more, its unhappy stones lie scattered upon the Galilean grass. Bethsaida, to your left upon the flat, where the upper Jordan pushes its delta into the north of the lake, had all the loveliness of Greece stamped upon it; and beyond again the string of white columns and walls in place after place along the eastern shore; in between and above them the groves of chestnut trees, on the heights the outlying Greek towns of the Decapolis.

On the extreme limit of your view, where the lake ceased, Tarichaeae, where the pickling of fish from the lake supported an industry which sent its delicacies all over the Roman world. Hidden between that point and the other great and noble town of Tiberias were the baths which the wealthy sought not only from all that country, but from far away, for their healing. Men counted nine towns at least, apart from intervening suburbs and villages, along that short ring of coastal land.

There in Capharnaum stood up the grandeur of the Great Synagogue, with its high Corinthian columns and the carving of the Manna in between.

It was in this building, majestic, with the outward order of Greece, consecrated within by the traditions and teaching of those who had maintained for centuries the worship of the Most High God, that Our Lord first proclaimed the Eucharist.

There, in the Great Synagogue of Capharnaum, to its crowded hall, were these strange words first said: "I am the living bread which came down from heaven. If any man eat of this bread he shall live for ever: and the bread that I will give is my flesh for the life of the world . . ."

Those strange words were said, and they were bewildering. In the buzz of talk arising on this could be discerned such a protest as this: "How can this man give us his flesh to eat?" But the silence that followed was broken by the reiterated words: "Except you eat the flesh of the

Son of Man and drink His blood you shall not have life in you."

If you turned, standing on that rising ground above the lake by Chorazain, and looked northward, you saw the snows of Hermon rising high into heaven nearly 10,000 feet above the lake, barely thirty miles away, and dominating all that land. On the flanks of that great mountain at its feet some twenty odd miles from where you stood, was the little paradise (as it then was) of Caesarea Philippi. There the living waters gushed out of the limestone with a wealth of greenery about them; the marble columns of a temple shone upon the cliff above, and the Greeks, delighting in so much beauty, dedicated the groves to Pan and to the Nymphs. Thence ran the great Roman road to Damascus.

It was here, in Caesarea Philippi, that loveliest corner of what was still then everywhere a lovely land, that the famous question was asked and answered, "Whom do you say that I am?" . . . "Thou art Christ, the Son of the living God." And here it was that openly and by a solemn published word the indestructible title of the Catholic Church was proclaimed: "I will build my church and the gates of Hell shall not prevail against it."

The site is symbolical. It is an origin in every way, is that very height of the Jordan valley. There stretches southward, past the lesser mere, then past the Sea of Galilee, then down the long trench to the Dead Sea, and the mass of bare stony heights which are Judea, all the scenes of this Story. Thence runs for its hundred and thirty miles the countryside on which all the future of the world from that day onwards has turned.

And thence it was that Our Lord turning His face

southwards towards all that land, began His journey to the
appointed end, to Jerusalem, to the Passion, and Death
upon the Cross.

Such was the setting of the story; such the Kingdom
of this World, as it moved past the Apostles in their
goings back and forth with their Master: everywhere the
might of a great culture and the splendour of its sculp-
tured stones and the wealth of its commerce and the crowds
of its superabundant people.

Stand on that same height and look around you today.
There is nothing. Magdala, the City of Pleasure, drawn
luxuriously along the shore, has utterly departed; a hut or
two and a bush. Great Capharnaum is the scattered stones
hidden in growth on which men dispute whether it was
really there or no; Chorazain is a doubtful name, a wretched
hamlet; a traditional low cliff may be, or is, the mark of
what was once Gesara. And Tiberias, itself once a high
city with three miles of walls, might be any one of the
squalid overgrown villages which the wreck of civilisation has left like flotsam behind it.

So utterly has the blight and devastation of the half-
barbaric conqueror reduced this land that even the names
of what was once so great have become obscure.

No story is more famous than that of the Gadarene
swine—yet only now are men, quite recently, fairly assured (but not yet quite assured) that the spelling is
erroneous; that the true place of the miracle was not
Gadara at all—how could it have been six miles from the
lake shore and cut off from it by the deep valley of the
Yarmuk?—but rather Gesara.

Men dispute on Bethsaida: stood it here or there?
Caesarea Philippi is not; the excellent title which Greek
fancy gave it—the Place of Pan, Paneas—is preserved in

Arabic corruption—"Banias," a fortress in ruins also; but of all the beauty and wealth that stood there, nothing.

The Decapolis to the east, the Greek cities, are (all save Damascus) a desolation; and the refrain perpetually recurring is the same everywhere—ruins . . . ruins . . . ruins.

The Lake

WHEN OUR LORD LEFT NAZARETH AND BEGAN HIS PUBLIC
predication, He went down first to the Sea of Galilee close
at hand. There it was he began to choose the Apostles;
there it was that the great Story openly began.

On this account the Sea of Galilee (which is also called
the Lake of Tiberias) has become the most famous sheet
of water in the world.

Nazareth itself stands in the folds of rolling highlands
which reach the height of from two to three thousand feet
above the sea, the highlands of Galilee. These hills are
the distinctive feature of the country, standing separate as
they do from the stony hills of Judea to the south; and
from them down to the lake shore (a matter as the crow
flies of fifteen miles but by the new road of seventeen) is
a drop of over 2,000 feet, over grassy country with here
and there a village, such as Cana of Galilee, within an
easy walk of Nazareth where Our Lord worked His first
miracle.

The road goes on, still falling, past the broad sward of
Hattin, where was fought one of the most important battles in history, the battle in which the Christians lost the
Holy Land, seven hundred and fifty years ago. It con-
tinues, the valley of the Upper Jordan opening before it,
and the deep hollow in which the Lake lies, its waters at
last apparent before you and the dark steep hills beyond,

which correspond upon the east of the Jordan trench to what the hills of Galilee are upon the west.

So at last, at the end of half a day downwards, you come to the shore at the place which gave the Sea of Galilee its Greek and Roman name: the town of Tiberias.

I know many others have spoken with enthusiasm of the beauty they found in this deep cup, buried between the opposing hills. It was not beauty which affected me when I saw it; the landscape is stern, and I will maintain of this great site as of all else southward, down to Bethlehem itself, of all else in this land save Nazareth, that it carries more air of tragedy than any other.

Mighty things were done, the greatest of spiritual victories and the triumph of the Resurrection at the end—but I can only believe that the Passion has chiefly imprinted itself upon all that land wherein Our Lord taught, gave the signs from Heaven, and suffered, at last, the Agony.

Though here, on this placid oval mirror of the Lake, placid save for those very sudden storms which rise and are gone sometimes in an hour, such storms as you always find in the enclosed waters of mountain lands, there is no name or spot recalling the mighty tragedy, yet that tragedy broods over it.

It was first the knowledge and personal experience, it was later, when that generation had died, the Faith, of Christian men, that the tragedy was succeeded by glory. And doubtless, to a full vision, all this land, from happy Nazareth in the north to Bethlehem, three days' journey away to the south, is lit, as by a sudden sunrise, with the Resurrection. It should be so. But to me as I first looked on that landscape it was not so, and I think would not be so were I to return there a hundred times. Rather the solemnity as of a profound horror, the sombre silence of the hill-sides that hang so awfully about it, were filled with a precognition of what was to come.

Here all the first wonders were wrought; here first from Magdala, a little northward along the shore, came the woman whose association with the Story will be spoken of till the end of the world. Here were the multitudes who heard the Voice, here, further to the north again, stood Capharnaum, which should be filled with memories of revelation, of the beginning of doctrine, of the appearance of the Kingdom of God, and with nothing else.

But we know, and not we alone, that all this was to fail very quickly in the eyes of the world. It was to last three years; it was to end in a local climax at Jerusalem; it was not to be of very great immediate fame; and the close was to be intolerable pain of body and the worst sufferings of the expectant mind—jeers and tortures and a dreadful death. The land has not escaped the stamp of that Deicide.

I note also that as the world progressed in its gradual apostasy, as doctrine faded from its intelligence, and as the meaning of all that was here done was lost to it, so did what is called "the modern mind" begin to sentimentalise over the landscape of Judea, and particularly over these waters of the Lake: insisting upon, exaggerating beauty; when it should rather have had before it the awful business which transformed the world.

And let me say this too—though I know I am here far from repeating what others have said whose eyes have fallen upon the sacred soil—there seems to me to be in a sense upon all the places of the Predication, the public life of Our Lord, and not only in Jerusalem, the living echo stamped upon it of the Lamentation which Jesus made over the walls of the city, foreseeing their destruction.

For Tiberias also, and all the places round about, bears that mood of desolation and ruin which fell upon the Holy Land when the lesser thing conquered the greater, and the men of the desert, with their new degraded heresy, swept over and destroyed the splendours inherited by Christendom from the old Pagan world, whence our civilisation came.

Tiberias was stately and splendid, with the Grecian column everywhere and the marble statuary and colonnades which you may still see overthrown, lying in ruins, of city after city from Palmyra in the desert to Petra in the far south. All that loveliness, all that dignity, has gone; and the squalor has replaced it which follows everywhere at last the sweep of the Mohammedan conquest.

Magdala has been wiped out; a few stones and a house or two of no presence, a tree or two, and the reeds along the lake are all that remain On the slope above stand the new villas of wealthy immigrant Jews. Capharnaum is not even a name. The Greek proportion and beauty, the Roman soldiery and order, the full life and wealth of that countryside, with its capital called after and, as it were, dedicated to the glory of the Empire and its head— all these have gone. And that feeling which oppresses every man who goes eastward of the Adriatic comes upon one almost fiercely here on these desolating shores. Ruins . . . ruins . . . ruins.

Yet in the midst of all this, appearing visionary above the physical emptiness of what was once so active and so filled, moves the profound pageantry of the opening Gospel. Here were the words first said (in Aramaic, it is believed, to the poorer people, but surely in Greek to many) which were the prelude. Their strength gives substance to the deserted places, and peoples the shore and the slopes above.

If you look eastward over the water you see within you the stilling of the storm, and also the Figure passing swiftly over the water to the astonished fishermen upon the boat. That boat, which was the poor possession of Cephas, called also Peter, is a vessel which can never founder; which shall not be cast upon a beach in age and broken up, as other vessels are.

The Sea of Galilee is today both bereft of life and filled with its presence. It is empty to the eye and silent to the ear, but a multitude fills it, and the splendour of palaces and temples, many cities, wealth, the noise of soldiers, and in that setting the unique and novel gem, on that field the sowing of the seed; on that platform the foundation of the Church.

About Wine

WINE IS OF SUCH DIVINITY THAT IT REFUSES TO CHANGE ITS name. It has kept the same name since it was first pupped, and though it is spelt differently in all sorts of languages (Greek which started it, Latin which carried it on and English where it still hangs on by the skin of its teeth, French where it has been terribly shortened and nasalized, Belgian where it carries a nice little 'g' subdued at the end of its name, and the German dialects in which it goes on being itself more or less—though the vowel has gone wrong, as vowels will), wine goes on being wine still. Mark my words, you my readers who are destined to live for ever, it will not change. What it was in the beginning that it will be. It is the steadfast thing of this world.

Wine, let me tell you, is unique, simple, not to be modified. It is wholly itself and of its own nature. When you play tricks with it, you change it not slightly but altogether. Hence also there is this about it: that being a chief Person in this world, it will be recognised for what it is or will not deal with you at all. It holds a regal state and is at once absolute and alone, yet perfectly satisfied with its own essence; for indeed wine is a god.

Those who are wise will remark that wine will only appear on blessed land, and there is not much of such land. Here in the Old World there is a belt, rather narrow, wherein the grape, which is the parent of wine, ripens to the glory of God and to the infinite benefit of mankind. But that belt will not run as far north as the Baltic or the Channel; beyond the Mediterranean it will not run far south of the Atlas. Just as the great vineyards are confined to a very small acreage of their own country, so is the soil and climate proper to wine confined to a small part of the habitable world. There is no wine in the Tropics; there is no wine in the Arctic; nor, indeed, for a long way south of the Arctic. There was, indeed, some sort of wine in England hundreds of years ago, but it died out after fighting hard for its life. I never heard of wine grown in Ireland, though the soul of the Irish is well suited to wine. When I wandered about in Poland some years ago, I found that wine was a foreign thing.

So wine is of its own territory, and that territory is select out of all the territories of the world. I have read that the Persians know wine and were the only Mohammedans who did; also there are famous Persian poems, one of them famously translated into English, which give the right glory to wine. But for the rest it is almost wholly of Europe and of civilized Europe. There is no wine in the Baltic plain, nor do the Prussians crush the grape. There is no wine in the vast spaces of Muscovy unless you include therein the happy corner of the Euxine Chersonese. There is no wine, I am told, in China nor among the Hindoos; nor any among the peoples of the Pacific, unless you count the Australians, who have, as we all know, planted vineyards and rigorously taken to winemaking. Wine is a part of the soul of Europe and proper to ourselves. When we find it in far-off places, the Cape or California, it is but a colony of ourselves.

Wine seems to me to be the test of things European. Were Europe—essential Europe—to perish, why, then, wine would perish too. But when wine disappears, it will be time for us to cover our faces and die; for without wine we shall not be ourselves any more. By wine came the column and the temple, the marble figures and the right colours, all that is permanent in the beauty man has created; and without wine that beauty would sink away.

Here in England the double fate which has for so many centuries disputed the English soul is discovered in the matter of wine. Wine was a necessity for whatever was cultivated in England; for the writers and the singers of England and the governors of England, the painters and builders of England, century after century; but it was not the familiar necessity of Englishmen at large. They preferred, when they were most themselves, a barley brew which the first writers on England, almost two thousand years ago, remarked in Kent and which you may (thank God) drink in Kent to this day. Quite lately they have taken, have the English, to many other things; and largely to alien strong waters, particularly to whisky, which came in from the outer lands. But wine still after a fashion survives among such Englishmen who are in tune with the ancient traditions of the island, and of its culture. They no longer drink it out of gold as was the royal custom of the Celtic chieftians, crying 'Vin ap or' (or some such horrible noise); they drink it out of glass, a fragile thing; though the wisest of them drink it out of silver, or silver-gilt which is better still; for I will ever maintain that the mere contact with gold provokes a response in wine, which, whenever it meets gold in any form, salutes a brother and a twin. On this account, in the days when we were allowed to have gold coins in England, it was the custom of some very few to cast a sovereign into any cup of wine before they took it to their lips, much as the baser sort will put sugar into tea.

It is pathetic but illuminating indeed to discover how

strongly the barbarian has sought and desired wine. He would come hundreds of miles over the angry seas to get it and it was one of the chief objects of his piracies. He was proud to acclimatize it, as much as could be, in his own lands; and sometimes it rewarded him by giving him a very special sort of revelation, producing certain wines which, though from far beyond the boundaries of the Empire, were still worthy of Christian men.

It has been said that 'Man Without Wine is an Ox.' Would that he were as much as that! He is something much worse than an ox when he lacks wine. He is a thief, a murderer, a fool and a raving despairing fellow; or, what is much lower, a washed-out nothing; an emptiness. For wine makes man much more surely than man makes wine. Put down a colony of men where you will and you cannot be sure that they will make wine. Indeed, the greater part of them fail hopelessly in the attempt, even when they desire to reach the glory of wine-makers. But though men do not always make wine, wine always makes men everywhere. Introduce it to half men, quarter men, and the great masses of No men, and it turns them into something newer, better, stronger, more permanent, more multiple, deeper rooted, of firmer fibre, better balanced and, in a word, *nourished*.

For who can be properly nourished, if indeed he be of human stock, without wine? St. Paul said to someone who had consulted him (without remembering that, unlike St. Luke, he was no physician), 'Take a little wine for your stomach's sake.' But I say, take plenty of it for the sake of your soul and all that appertains to the soul: scholarship, verse, social memory and the continuity of all culture. There may be excess in wine; as there certainly is in spirits and champagne, but in wine one rarely comes across it; for it seems to me that true wine rings a bell and tells you when you have had enough. But there is certainly such a thing as a deficiency of wine; and such deficiency is one of the most awful ravenous beasts that can fasten upon a living soul. To drink an insufficient portion of wine, leaving the whole being, body and soul, craving for a full portion, is torture. The feeling of loss will pursue a man for hours. On this account our fathers were wont to leave their guests at liberty to call for wine according to their desire; and you may read in any old book, written in the days when England was England, how men called for wine at the table of a host as though that table were their own. Pray heaven this wholesome custom shall return. But like other civilized things it can only come back after great travail and strain; for our vagaries and negligence have already three-quarters ruined us.

I call that man fortunate who, looking back over a long life (such as mine has been), can mark the various stages of his travel by experience in wine. He will say to himself, as he turns over in his soul the memories of youth and of better times, 'Soul, do you remember the wine we drank on that hillside overlooking the Rhine in the better days? Soul, was it not on the Upper Ebro that you and I sat together with a companion wine strong and rough but nobly a friend? Soul, do you remember how, in the midst of Sicily, fainting from fatigue, a goddess came upon you, sent to you for your deliverance, and bearing a pitcher of wine which had been drawn for the gods who were carousing in a neighbouring room? Soul, have you forgotten a certain wine of Touraine which stamped itself upon history for ever, although no record of it has been written down? Soul, are you so ungrateful as to recall no more that wine which had been born in a lonely valley of Jura Hills and made the spot hallowed *in aeternum*? Soul, will you not retain the benediction of a certain flask produced for you by a kindly crone in the Lower Apennine, whereby this aged dame earned, and shortly after received, her entry into paradise (for when I passed that way a year later, she was in glory)?' To all these rhetorical questions the soul replies with enthusiastic gratitude, affirming that it never has and never will forget these revelations granted to it during its little passage through the daylight.

Now at the mention of these words, 'its little passage through the daylight,' I am reminded of a story which I have told by word of mouth perhaps a thousand times, and even in print too often; but it is better to repeat a good thing than to let it die. The young curate said to the bishop as he lay in his last illness, 'My lord, I have brought you a glass of that wine.' The young curate then kneeling by the bed of his venerable patron burst into tears and added, 'Oh, my lord! Soon you will be drinking other and better wine in another and a better world!' To this the hierarch replied, little above a whisper, 'In a better world my faith constrains me to believe, but a better wine than this could never be.' And this, note you, was said of common port. What would he have said had they given him just when it was ripe, just when it was loudest in its praises to the Lord God, the wine of whats-its-name of the year whatever-it-was, which all just men of sufficient experience know to be the greatest wine of the greatest moment in the history of mankind? But the name of that vintage and its date I will not publish until I see my way to earning an adequate reward for the advertisement.

All have heard the true and sufficient story of the younger man who said to the elder man, 'How does one tell good wine?' To whom the elder answered, 'By the taste.' Would that the whole world could learn the lesson of that famous reply. It is not the year, nor the vineyard that distinguishes good wine, exceptional wine. It is the taste. There is no red wine so excellent that you cannot kill it and turn it into vinegar by warming it excessively and too quickly. There is no white wine so remarkable that you cannot destroy it by drinking it after the wrong meats. There is no wine that ever was which remains the same if you leave it open too long. In other words, there is no wine that is itself alone; for all wine, like all human character (of which wine is the reflection and the symbol), is conditioned by circumstance.

Men lay up store of many things, principally of money or the equivalent thereof. Some even lay up store of wisdom; and some, much fewer, of human affection, which is really a most valuable commodity. But few today lay up a store of wine with any knowledge, discretion, choice, intention or continuity. It used to be the common habit with all men who were worthy to consume wine; but in the general decline of the world that habit is dying out. No man can build what is called a cellar and maintain it without constant attention to one home; and most men are too poor to enjoy the same home long, for most men today have been turned into pauper vagrants. No man can make a cellar who is not prepared to watch unceasingly the ingoing and the outgoing; for this excellence is no more static than any other human excellence. Change and mortality overshadow even wine. There are other dangers and impossibilities about the making of a store of wine. It needs the right temperature constantly maintained; it needs protection against violence and vibration; it needs a sort of unending diary or chart of its daily progress. Few would ever be at such pains in the past and today hardly any.

Yet I suppose that the making of a just and adequate wine-treasure will not be wholly abandoned and that somewhere in the ends of the earth, in a dale of Northumberland or perhaps a forgotten village of Cornwall, I shall come again upon a man who has nursed, cherished and preserved an inheritance of wine. There were many such men when I was young, especially here in England. There were many also in Belgium. Such men seem indeed to be proper to territories that have no wine of their own, for what we lack we remember and we prize.

On this account also I trust that the grave peril now hanging over us, lest continual war should destroy the continuity of wine, will make men consider again the imperative duty of saving and handing on to those who shall come after us this greatest of material things, wine.

I am willing to believe that for what is irreplaceable there is a special providence: for good verse that rarest of flowers; for certain landscapes threatened by the greed of men; for certain songs of country people. I willingly believe, therefore, that true wine itself shall not perish either through the degradation of mankind or through oblivion. But, alas, I am none too sure.